Praise for *Miracle Minded Manager*

. . . .

"*Miracle Minded Manager* is far more than a book on management. It is a book on life. Through his gifted storytelling, John Murphy describes how to achieve peace and happiness outside the office, and at the same time, he artfully explains how to take those concepts into the workplace to build a stronger, more collaborative culture and team that achieves great results with reduced stress. I have urged my family to read it. I cannot give it a higher endorsement."

—**Gary Garfield**, keynote speaker and retired chairman, president, and CEO of Bridgestone Americas, Inc.

"John Murphy goes beyond standard business models to a completely different level—the only level at which real, lasting change takes place. *Miracle Minded Manager* uses the principles of *A Course in Miracles*, which has healed millions of lives . . . A must-read for anyone who wants to improve their business or their life in general."

—**Lorri Coburn**, MSW, author of *Breaking Free* and coeditor *A Course in Miracles And . . .*

"In *Miracle Minded Manager*, John Murphy offers an intriguing and compelling story about how a man and his family turn their stressful and mundane lives into the miraculous. This book is for everyone wanting to maneuver through daily stress to live with more peace and joy. What a perfect message for these times."

—**Marci Shimoff**, #1 *New York Times* bestselling author of *Happy for No Reason* and *Chicken Soup for the Woman's Soul*

"This book has come at the perfect time. In an intriguing and brilliant manner, John Murphy offers us a profound alternative; a true paradigm shift in the field of leadership and human behavior. Thank you, John, for giving us this book."

—**Dr. Marshall Goldsmith**, *New York Times* bestselling author of *Triggers*, *MOJO*, and *What Got You Here Won't Get You*; *Thinkers50* #1 executive coach

"As author John Murphy states so aptly in this monumental book, 'It often takes a certain amount of suffering before people are ready to challenge the ego and open up to the Truth.' Before your personal suffering becomes too great, I urge you to join Jack, the *Miracle Minded Manager*, on his miraculous journey to discovering how anyone can live true success, happiness, and most of all, peace of mind."

—**Debra Poneman**, bestselling author and founder of *Yes to Success* Seminars, Inc.

"*Miracle Minded Manager* delivers a true-life look into the daily issues each of us face and provides a practical road map for helping every business executive improve their culture from fear-based to inspired and fearless."

—**Dan Barcheski**, founder and CEO of Axios HR

"John writes with passion, ingenuity, and remarkable intuition to give us profound insights on how to live happier, healthier, more peaceful lives. I highly recommend this book to anyone seeking more inner peace, awareness, and equanimity—in and outside the business world."

—**Janet Bray Attwood**, *New York Times* bestselling author of *The Passion Test* and *Your Hidden Riches*

"We need the lessons in *Miracle Minded Manager* now more than ever. I am so very grateful for this book and the work John is doing."

—**A. P. "Skip" Aldridge III**, founder, president, and CEO of Head of Sales Consulting, Inc. and former senior executive at Pharmavite, ConAgra Foods, and Del Monte Foods

"John Murphy's book *Miracle Minded Manager* is a great read and provides a provocative system that balances the material world of business with your soul."

—**Lynn Andrews**, *New York Times* bestselling author of the *Medicine Woman* series

"*Miracle Minded Manager* offers those in business a new way of looking at the world and a revolutionary system of thought and action. It's a practical approach to business using the Course."

—**David Hoffmeister**, author of *Awakening through A Course in Miracles*

"*Miracle Minded Manager* is a manual on living a happy and purpose-filled life in business and beyond. I highly recommend this book to business teams, individuals, and even families who want to bring more peace, collaboration and organization to their business and their life."

—**Britney Shawley**, founder and CEO of Whole & Healthy Kitchens and visionary and teacher at Miracles of Mind

"Several years ago, I contracted John Murphy to help me lead a major culture change. The insight, ingenuity, and practical applications that he brought to my team and our organization of over 50,000 associates was truly inspirational. It is no wonder he is now teaching, and writing, Miracle Minded management. John is an excellent teacher, writer, and coach who walks his talk. I think *Miracle Minded Manager* is his best work yet. It is a quick read and yet it makes you stop and think—a lot! I found it fascinating and will continue to use the lessons for the rest of my life."

—**John Ayala**, president of ADP

Praise for **John Murphy's** Books

• •

"I have read, absorbed and reviewed hundreds of spiritual enlightenment books. I have searched, journeyed, and transcended. However, until *Beyond Doubt*, I did not know quite how to put it all together."

—**Shirley Roe**, *Allbooks Review*, Toronto

"The ability to change and adapt in today's world is critical to success. John Murphy's book *Agent of Change* does an outstanding job detailing how we can lead people and organizations through change. I highly recommend this book to anyone desiring to improve their personal leadership skills."

—**Peter F. Secchia**, chairman of Universal Forest Products and former US Ambassador to Italy

"John Murphy is one of my all-time favorite authors. He is brilliant, and *Zentrepreneur* is a must-read for any leader or anyone wanting to start a business."

—**Mac Anderson**, founder of Successories and Simple Truths

"Reengineering isn't just about changing corporate systems and structures. It's about getting people to feel more autonomy and ownership in what they do. That's what I like about John Murphy's book *Reinvent Yourself*. It focuses on change at the personal level. I highly recommend it."

—**Dr. Denis Waitley**, author of *The Psychology of Winning*

"*Agent of Change* is a book for anyone who is trying to change things, whether it be at work, home, or in the community. Let John Murphy be your guide through the minefields that accompany any change effort."

—**Dr. Ken Blanchard**, coauthor of *The One Minute Manager*

"There is a book I want you to read. As a syndicated columnist, I regularly get books sent to me, often several in a week. I look through them all, hoping to find a gem . . . and I have! It's John Murphy's *Reinvent Yourself*. What I admired most about the book is that it captured the relationship between work, personality and family. It is heartwarming and soulful and a good read."

—**Dale Dauten**, author of *The Max Strategy* (quote excerpted from the *Chicago Tribune*, syndicated by King Features)

"You must and will change. This book, *Agent of Change*, will help you do it properly."

—**Richard M. DeVos**, cofounder of Amway Corporation

"I can't help but tell you how much I enjoyed *Reinvent Yourself*. The easy storytelling style made it a real page-turner. I think we all need to continually reinvent ourselves, so thanks for giving us the outline to do just that. Keep up the good work! You are making a difference!"

—**Rocky Bleier**, four-time Super Bowl winner

A Modern-Day Parable about How to Apply
A Course in Miracles in Business

MIRACLE
MINDED
MANAGER

JOHN J. MURPHY

BEYOND WORDS
Hillsboro, Oregon

BEYOND WORDS

8427 N.E. Cornell Road, Suite 500
Hillsboro, Oregon 97124-9808
503-531-8700 / 503-531-8773 fax
www.beyondword.com

Managing Editor: Lindsay S. Easterbrooks-Brown
Copyeditor: Kristin Thiel, Emmalisa Sparrow Wood
Proofreader: Madison Schultz
Interior design: Devon Smith
Composition: William H. Brunson Typography Services

First Beyond Words paperback edition October 2019

BEYOND WORDS PUBLISHING and colophon are registered trademarks of Beyond Words
Publishing, Inc. Beyond Words is an imprint of Simon & Schuster, Inc.

For information about special discounts for bulk purchases, please contact Beyond Words Special
Sales at 503-531-8700 or specialsales@beyondword.com.

Manufactured in the United States of America

10 9 8 7 6 5 4 3 2 1

Library of Congress Cataloging-in-Publication Data

Names: Murphy, John, author.
Title: Miracle minded manager : a modern-day parable about how to apply
  a course in miracles in business / John Murphy.
Description: Hillsboro, Oregon : Beyond Words, [2019]
Identifiers: LCCN 2019003864 (print) | LCCN 2019981413 (ebook) | ISBN
  9781582707174 (paperback) | ISBN 9781582707259 (ebook)
Subjects: LCSH: Leadership. | Self-actualization (Psychology) | Spiritual life.
Classification: LCC HD57.7 .M8678 2019 (print) | LCC HD57.7 (ebook) | DDC
  658.4/09—dc23
LC record available at https://lccn.loc.gov/2019003864
LC ebook record available at https://lccn.loc.gov/2019981413

The corporate mission of Beyond Words Publishing, Inc.: *Inspire to Integrity*

Nothing real can be threatened. Nothing unreal exists.
Herein lies the peace of God.

—*A Course in Miracles*

Contents

CONTENTS

CONTENTS

What is the relation of [contemplation] to action?
Simply this. He who attempts to act and do things
for others or for the world without deepening his own
self-understanding, freedom, integrity, and capacity
to love will not have anything to give others. He will
communicate to them nothing but the contagion of
his own obsessions, his aggressiveness, his ego-
centered ambitions, his delusions about ends and means,
his doctrinaire prejudices and ideas. There is nothing
more tragic in the modern world than the misuse
of power and action.

—Thomas Merton

Preface

The Time is Now

> An unexamined life is not worth living.
>
> —Socrates

Prepare yourself. Your life is about to change. Mine certainly has. And it has changed because of what you are about to read.

For the past thirty years I have built a successful management consulting firm by being different. Unlike most of the business leaders and consultants I have met, I am not afraid, and people sense it. They even ask me about it. "Does nothing bother you? Don't you get nervous?"

I started my company at the age of twenty-eight with very little knowledge—or certainty—and have since done work for hundreds of organizations in dozens of countries, including the United States military and several *Fortune 500* companies. My job is to teach business leaders how to pull people together as a team, develop highly effective strategies, improve performance, and boost results. Often, I am going into these organizations alone and teaching high-profile leaders how to get out of their own way. There is simply no way I could do this successfully if I was afraid.

This was not always the case. Like any human being, growing up, I was frequently anxious and stressed about one thing or another. I remember one time when I was giving a speech to my high school—I was so nervous I almost got sick. The same was true before stepping onto the football field as a quarterback, both in high school and at the University of Notre Dame. Wasn't anxiety normal? Couldn't I just fake it until I make it? Now I give speeches all over the world.

Growing up in a Catholic family, I was taught about faith, but what I learned later is that one cannot have true faith and be afraid at the same time. It is one or the other. Period. True faith does not come and go. It is a complete thought-system, as is fear. In retrospect, I thought I had faith, but this was an illusion. I was under the influence of the fear-based, ego thought-system: Seek and ye shall *not* find. There is always something wrong. People are out to get you. What if you screw up? *Faith* was a popular word but a nearly impossible practice. At the time, I assumed the best I could do was find ways to manage the stress with things like exercise, meditation, and positive thinking.

In 2009 I worked through *A Course in Miracles* (ACIM) for the first time. Since that time, not a day has gone by that I do not reflect on the profound lessons and insights gained from this 365-day course. I now continue to use *ACIM* to guide me as a business consultant, speaker, teacher, writer, husband, father, son, brother, and leadership development coach.

When I first learned of the course, I was intrigued with many self-help books, lectures, videos, audios, and credible teachers—anything that could help me "up my game." In fact, I had already written eight books at the time and shared the stage with inspirational speakers Tony Robbins, Zig Ziglar, Jim Rohn, General H. Norman Schwarzkopf, Denis Waitley, Rocky Bleier, and many others. I was eager and hungry for knowledge and tips on how to help people around the world live a more inspiring and meaningful life, including me.

When I continued to hear references to *ACIM* from Eckhart Tolle, Deepak Chopra, David Hawkins, Marianne Williamson, Wayne Dyer, and others, I decided to investigate. As it turns out, it was quite easy for me to do this because one day an invitation to *ACIM* was seeking me out in my mail. I responded immediately. This was no coincidence. This was synchronicity.

The course was developed in the 1970s over a seven-year period. Helen Schucman, an agnostic, Jewish psychologist at Columbia University, channeled a "voice" into what now consists of the three parts to *ACIM*: a text, a 365-day workbook—one lesson per day for a year—and a teacher's manual. As you can imagine, Helen was quite reluctant and afraid at first, but with the help of a colleague, Bill Thetford, she "took notes," and together, Helen and Bill developed the course, which was then published by the Foundation for Inner Peace. Today, many scholars around the world consider the "voice" to be that of Jesus and the teachings to be truly profound and enlightening.

Since I was very passionate about learning "secrets" to success far beyond superficial outcomes, I had been studying and experimenting with a variety of spiritual teachings over many years, ranging from those of Jesus to the Buddha to Lao Tzu and the Tao. *ACIM* fit in perfectly. As I see it now, there are no inconsistencies in true spirituality, and the "experiences" one can have by applying the lessons in *ACIM* are nothing short of true miracles. I eagerly took these insights and learnings into my business consulting practice, writings, and teachings, and there is no doubt it has had a profound effect on my life and the lives of the people and the organizations I serve. Now I no longer try to manage or cope with stress. I simply don't feel it. And if it does try to creep back into my life, I recognize the root cause (which is a self-projected illusion), and I dismiss it. How freeing is that!

Miracle Minded Manager combines and integrates spirituality and business leadership like no other book. Relatively few people consider miracles and management as an important mix. My intention with this book is to share an entertaining and compelling story (a sequel to my book *Agent of Change: Leading a Cultural Revolution*), showing you how to apply lessons and insights from *ACIM* and other spiritual teachings through fictional characters in a common business setting.

As a backdrop, *Agent of Change*, originally published in 1994, allows readers to listen in on some fascinating and enlightening conversations between two characters, Jack MacDonald, the general manager of a division of TYPCO (Typical Company), and Jordan McKay, an intriguing business consultant. With the help of Jordan, Jack learns how to overcome a great deal of resistance to completely reinvent the organizational culture he leads. In addition to this, he learns valuable insights that apply to his personal life.

This experience is not easy for Jack. Frequently, he is frustrated and at a loss for answers. When he asks Jordan for straight answers, he is left with Socratic riddles and more questions. Jordan's extraordinary teaching style parallels that of many spiritual mystics seeking to help people get out of their own way. Ultimately, Jack learns how to think differently, and the lights begin coming on in very practical ways. Little does he know that Jordan had to learn much of this the hard way. And Jack has a lot more to learn himself!

ACIM is never mentioned in the book *Agent of Change* and it is not necessary to read *Agent of Change* before reading this book. It is only now in this sequel that Jack learns of the course and begins to apply it himself, leading to a whole new level of understanding, awareness, empowerment, and appreciation in life. Welcome to *Miracle Minded Manager*.

—John Murphy

The privilege of a lifetime is to become who you truly are.

—C. G. Jung

PART ONE

The Ego Thought-System

My cup runneth over.

— **Psalm 23:5**

1

An Intelligent Fool

Any intelligent fool can make things bigger and more complex.
It takes a touch of genius and a lot of courage to move
in the opposite direction.

—E. F. Schumacher

I sit quietly at my desk, shaking my head in frustration. Despite my success leading another division of TYPCO through a major cultural revolution, I feel like I'm back at square one. The business unit I lead now as president is bigger, broader, and probably more dysfunctional than anything I have ever seen. We offer more products and more services with more people to more customers, and many of our customers are not happy. Our Net Promoter Score (NPS), which is a tool we use to measure customer satisfaction, is very low and even negative in several categories. That means we have more unhappy customers, or detractors, than delighted customers, or promoters. The number of phone calls coming into our customer service department each day is alarming, so all I tend to hear is that we need more service reps, more telephones, and we need more training and space. A few of my key managers are even lobbying to open a new call center overseas where we can get cheaper labor.

I glance at my email inbox. What a mess! I am back to the dependency syndrome we suffered from at my old division. Associates all over the company are delegating problems up to management rather than taking responsibility to solve them. Escalate this. Escalate that. I hate that word *escalate*. Our organization is so siloed and divided and hierarchical we seem to take ten steps to do something that could be done in two.

None of this is new to me, though. I had the same problem with my other division before I met Jordan McKay and we shook things up. Of course, that meant I had to make some tough decisions, including the dismissal of my friend, Wayne Peterson, who was our plant manager. Wayne just refused to change his negative behavior, and he became a barrier to the changes we needed to make. Fortunately, Wayne has now reinvented himself, with some help, and he is much happier. Maybe it's time for me to reinvent myself.

As I stare at my overloaded inbox, I am reminded of my challenges with Wayne. Only now it seems like I have multiple Waynes in the business unit, beginning with the guy in charge of business transformation, Joe Mulligan. How unfortunate. I'm not sure Joe knows what he is doing. On the one hand, he is well educated, and his credentials look great on paper. But on the other hand, we aren't seeing the changes I expect to see. And Joe isn't modeling the desired behavior we need to lead the transformation. He would rather study the situation than take a risk and change it. We have a severe case of analysis paralysis. No doubt about it. Meanwhile, fear, negativity, cynicism, resistance, comparison, and win-lose competition are still rampant throughout the organization, beginning with Joe. Finger-pointing and blame between divisions and departments is out of control. Sometimes I feel like I might have to fire half of my executive team to even begin a culture change. After all, culture reflects the leadership, starting with me and the team I inherited when I moved into this job. But firing a bunch of senior managers isn't realistic. I don't have much depth on the bench, which is another reflection of poor leadership. And bringing in a bunch of consultants isn't the answer in this case either. This business unit has been doing that for years under Joe's guidance, and it's still a mess. An expensive mess.

As I read through the first email, which happens to be from Joe, I can feel my blood pressure rising. I don't know what it is, but he just gets under my skin. He seems to complicate the simplest things. This email, for example, is three paragraphs long with several attachments. How in the world does someone like that get into a business transformation role responsible for making things lean? I am reminded of a quote from E. F. Schumacher, who said, "Any intelligent fool can make things bigger and more complex. It takes a touch of genius and a lot of courage to move in the opposite direction." Joe is an intelligent fool. We need to simplify, and he keeps making things bigger and more complex.

My mind drifts to Jordan and the work we did at my prior division. I could bring Jordan in to help change things like I did before, but something tells me I need to take charge of this myself. The last thing we need right now is another consultant, even if it is Jordan. Then I think about my options. What choices do I have? How am I supposed to delegate to people who don't know what they're doing? That seems to have gotten us to where we are now. Joe has had plenty of time to streamline things and generate more flow in the business. He simply hasn't done it.

I start writing Joe a response to his email, beginning with the word *no*. I then pause and laugh. Maybe I should just end my response here and hit send. That would be different. Normally, I respond in kind. One long email follows another. It's part of our current culture. We are so over-emailed at TYPCO it isn't funny. Joe is writing me to get my approval to do another major study and I am about to email him back saying no. Round and round we will go with nothing changing. I lean back in my chair and take a deep breath. Maybe I should contact Jordan. The stress of this new job is killing me.

I glance over at a picture of my family on the credenza. It's a framed photograph of my wife, Judy, and our two children, Kevin and Kathleen, taken several years ago when we were hiking in Breckenridge, Colorado. The smiles on our faces say a lot. We used to do things like that all the time. Hikes. Ski trips. Bicycle adventures. Island excursions. In fact, I even competed in a few mini-triathlons and 10K races. Believe it or not, I was in pretty good shape.

When I turn back to my computer, the screen has gone dark, and I catch a glimpse of my reflection. What a sight! I've easily gained twenty-five pounds since that photo was taken, and the idea of running a 10K makes me feel nauseous. My cheeks are chubby. My chin is starting to double up. My hair is thinning, and my hairline is receding. There are several deep wrinkles now etched across my forehead, like rivers flowing through a canyon, and it looks like a permanent scowl is forming around my mouth. I've got crow's feet growing around my eyes, which look tired and cloudy, masking the light and spark I remember seeing in my youth. It's no wonder. I haven't had a good night's sleep in months. I'm up at least two or three times a night just to pee. And then I have trouble falling back to sleep with all the pressures of work on my mind. My doctor tells me I'm okay but cautions me about my elevated blood pressure, which hasn't changed in two years, despite the medications I'm on.

I sigh. It seems now I hardly spend any quality time with my family. Kevin is away at college. Kathleen is busy navigating her way through high school. Judy is working full-time at a hospital. And I feel like I'm under a microscope here at TYPCO with the CEO and the board of directors watching my every move. They promoted me to deliver results immediately. No excuses. And they're paranoid about taking any significant risks or losing market value. What do they think I am? A miracle worker? Ugh, it feels like I'm on a treadmill to nowhere, without the benefits of exercise.

I wonder how Jordan handled this kind of pressure. That was one of the things that impressed me most about him. Before going into consulting, he had a similar role to the one I'm in now. He was president and CEO of a very large company. Clearly, he can relate to the relentless pressure and stress I'm going through. Yet he always seems so relaxed and confident, like he knows something the rest of the world is missing. Maybe he has a few more tips I can use. Clearly, I need help. I just don't want to admit it. What could it hurt to call him? I abandon Joe's email and grab my phone.

2

My True Competition

We have met the enemy, and he is us.

—made popular by Walt Kelly and
his character Pogo

Jordan McKay and I were introduced three years ago at a workshop in Boston. The topic was teamwork, and at that time, my division of TYPCO was anything but a healthy team. It was as if the right hand didn't know what the left hand was doing, and I was responsible for pulling people together. That was the title of Jordan's workshop—Pulling Together.

At first, I thought we needed some senior management team training. That's why I was investigating his seminar. I had heard good things about Jordan, so I decided to check him out for myself. Apparently, he was testing me as well. During our introductions, when I explained my intentions and expectations for being there, he quickly challenged me. He suggested we needed more than team training. Teamwork isn't something you *train* into a culture, he said. It is something you *design* into a culture. Training people on teamwork and then putting them back into a messed-up, dysfunctional system is an insult.

As it turns out, he was right. We needed an organizational overhaul. I remember him saying, "If you want to change the way you do things around here, you have to change the way you do things around here." For a minute I thought I was listening to Gandhi. In other words, if you want to change your *culture*—which is the way you do things—you must change your systems, policies, and structure—which is synonymous with the way you do things. Most people operate in whatever system you give them. If the system is messed up, training will do little good. It's like solving problems inside a box when it's the box itself that is the problem.

Jordan gave me a lot to think about that day, and he continued to help me over the next two years. My team made tremendous progress as a division of TYPCO, and as a result, I was promoted from general manager to president of one of our major business units. Little did I know that my life wasn't going to get any better. How ironic, I remember thinking. My business gets better, but my life seems to get worse. Now I have more anxiety and stress than ever before. Sure, I'm making more money, and I have more status. But I can't help but think about what it's costing me in terms of life balance, health, family, and the freedom to do what I want when I want.

When I called Jordan a few days ago to set up this meeting, he promised he would share more about his own stresses and life-changing experiences. It was a somewhat odd dialogue, but I now expect that from him. He tends to leave me hanging. I remember him quoting some ancient Eastern proverb: "When the student is ready, the teacher will appear." He was probably testing me again. Ready for what?

The small French café where we are meeting is ideal for personal conversations. It features quiet tables and booths, natural lighting, elegant artwork, and an abundance of vigorous plants. The menu is simple with fresh, healthy, organic offerings, herbal teas, and great coffee. The aroma is rich and inviting. Jordan says he loves it. I do too. This is where we met following the workshop three years ago, and it has grown on me. It feels very peaceful and welcoming.

As I look across the table, I notice Jordan's piercing blue eyes haven't changed a bit since the day we met. There is a light and an intelligence and a radiance that shine through them even when he is somber and serious. He also has a sense of fearlessness and optimism that I have never seen before. It's almost magnetic. I wonder where his confidence, equanimity, and inner peace are coming from. I could sure use some of that right now.

"So, you're feeling a bit stressed and overwhelmed at work," he says, recapping our telephone conversation. "Welcome to the club."

I laugh. "What club is that? The Stress Club?"

He smiles. "You might call it that."

"To my knowledge, the only club I belong to these days is a health club I rarely go to. Can't you tell by looking at me?"

Jordan doesn't flinch. He just sits there patiently, sipping his tea, as if waiting for me to open my mind and truly listen. He has cautioned me in the past about making excuses.

"Okay," I add curiously, now leaning back in my chair. "Enlighten me."

He sets his tea cup on the table and leans forward. "It isn't exactly a club as most people would define it. I simply use this metaphor because it helps people understand a form of suffering that often goes unnoticed. You even hinted at it just now when you revealed you belong to a health club, which requires dues, but you rarely go. You're invested in it, and yet you're getting no positive return. Let me ask you, Jack. How does this make you feel?"

I shift in my seat. "Like I'm getting ripped off, I suppose."

"Do you feel any shame or guilt when you think about it?"

"Yeah, I do. I get upset with myself because I'm neglecting my health and wasting money."

"What about apathy and grief?" he continues, as if following a script. "Do you feel any sense of hopelessness or despair or cynicism when you think about it?"

I reflect on my situation. "Yeah, sometimes it seems hopeless. I keep thinking that tomorrow will be different. I set new goals, including fitness goals, but they always seem to take a back seat to my work. I always seem to run out of time."

He appears to be listening carefully to what I'm saying, now sitting back contemplatively and scratching his chin. "Does this scare you in any way?"

I am just about to jump in and say no, but I stop myself. I want to think about this for a moment. It seems I am habitually conditioned to reject the idea of fear and insecurity or at least not admit it. All my life I've been trained to fake it until I make it. No one wants a fearful leader. I remember my dad telling me this when I was just a kid. But maybe deep down I am afraid. Maybe I am worried about my health and a whole lot of other things. I take a drink of my coffee. My father is now suffering from heart disease, and this certainly weighs on me. I have high blood pressure, which is clearly not ideal. Maybe I am a bit anxious about my health and family.

"I suppose it does scare me a little bit," I confess. "I do tend to worry about things."

"Sounds familiar," he replies. "And you said earlier that you get upset with yourself for neglecting your health and wasting money. You sense a deficiency, and this can trigger anger."

"Yeah, that's about right. I get angry from time to time, especially when I see injustice."

He shrugs. "Like I said, Jack, welcome to the club. The ego club. The club of human suffering. The club of shame, guilt, apathy, grief, fear, lust, anger, and pride."

Do I really belong to some mysterious club, paying dues of some sort and getting nothing but shame and guilt and grief in return? No wonder I feel stressed.

He continues. "Like I said before, the idea of a club is just a metaphor. To be more exact, you belong to a system, a thought-system, the ego thought-system, and you have a lot invested in it. This is a very common way of seeing the world and thinking and behaving in the world."

"The ego thought-system?" I question.

"Yes. It's a mind-set we are all familiar with as human beings. It is fear-based, protective, and dualistic in nature. It values separation and pride. It shows us that there is a right and a wrong, a good and a bad, an us and a them, a win and a lose dichotomy all around us. It is judgmental in nature and never satisfied. It is always comparing things—and people. The ego mantra is 'seek and ye shall not find.' No matter what you do or what you accomplish in life, the ego wants more. The grass is always greener somewhere else."

"Sounds like living in hell, the way you put it," I mutter, shifting again in my chair and crossing my arms.

"That's true, Jack," he replies quietly. "The ego does not know inner peace and heaven. In fact, it's the very barrier to inner peace and heaven. It's what separates us from our Source of well-being."

"What does that mean?" I interrupt. "Are you saying I'm going to hell?"

"No," he explains. "I'm not saying that at all. Hell is not a place, and neither is heaven. They are states of mind, states of consciousness. Given what you have just described to me, you are already living in hell."

I start to say something but stop myself. I've heard this before—that heaven isn't a destination but a kingdom within us. I sit silently, contemplating what Jordan is telling me.

He continues. "Let me share a quote with you from the mystic Rumi. He said, 'Out beyond ideas of wrongdoing and rightdoing, there is a field. I'll meet you there.'" He sips his tea. "Does this mean anything to you?"

"I suppose it means that we tend to get caught up in dualistic thinking and judging—which can be very upsetting," I surmise. "But I can't say I agree with Rumi. Of course there is right and wrong."

"According to who . . . or what? The ego?"

I sit patiently, trying to understand this bizarre quote and this unusual man. A field beyond right and wrong? Where is that?

"The field is heaven," he continues, as if reading my mind. "It's a field of energy, a state of inner peace, here and now, forever present. But the ego won't let us see it because it is threatened by it. Think of the ego as a form of denial and resistance. It exists to protect itself as a thought-system. And it is this resistance that blinds us from the Truth. It blinds us from knowing who we truly are—our capital S authentic Self."

"Is that why the ego is often referred to as the false self?"

"Yes, the ego casts a shadow that is often denoted as the false self. It is the ego that would have you think you are unworthy or unsafe," Jordan says. "Just remember something. God does not make mistakes. Everything in the universe is in perfect yin-yang harmony and balance."

I shake my head. "But what about the horrific things some people do? What about terrorists and rapists and criminals?"

"Great question," he replies. "In fact, it sounds a lot like the excuses, denial, and resistance I first had when I learned about awakening and transcendence. They should be condemned, right?" I'm about to say, "Hell yes," when I catch myself. Maybe this is the attack-and-defend mind-set Jordan is talking about. Maybe this is the ego "box" I'm in—the club of human suffering.

"Let me put it this way, Jack," he explains. "The ego believes in condemnation, which fuels guilt and stress at the subconscious level. Remember this: What goes around, comes around. When we judge the world, we judge ourselves. When we criticize the world, we criticize ourselves. When we doubt the world, we doubt ourselves. When we condemn the world, we condemn ourselves. Most people don't realize this consciously because it's happening at the subconscious level. As a result, we belong to a club, and we don't even know it. We're asleep, and we don't know it. We can blame the outside world all we want, but we are imprisoning ourselves by accepting this thought-system. Therefore, it is we who must free ourselves by transcending it, by letting it go. The power of decision is ours. Think of this as awakening from a bad dream."

"This club doesn't sound much like a health club." I sigh.

"Yes, that's why I said awakening from a *bad* dream. The ego thought-system is anything but a health club. Shame and guilt and grief are not healthy energies. Nor are fear and doubt and anxiety. Stress weakens the immune system and leaves our bodies more vulnerable to illness and disease."

"No wonder people get sick when they're stressed," I add, thinking of my dad.

"Yes, and there are all kinds of scientific data to back this up. If it makes you feel any better about not going to the gym, consider this: The key to good health requires a lot more than exercise and diet. It requires inner peace."

"Come to think of it, I do see a lot of frustrated and stressed people at the gym when I get my butt over there."

"Yes. These folks mean well, but they belong to the same club you do. And I'm not talking about the same gym. They are trying to *manage* stress rather than eliminate it. They're trying to solve a problem inside a box when it's the box that is the problem."

"Ha, I remember you saying that before. It's like people moving chairs around on the Titanic to make it look better. They don't see the iceberg."

Jordan sits back in his chair and finishes his tea. His eyes continue to gaze at me. I don't know what it is about this man, but there is something very engaging about him, even though he ticks me off sometimes. He continues, "And since it's the box, or mental programming, that is the problem, the only way to eliminate stress is to transcend the thought-system that is projecting it. A shift at this level changes everything. You see, stress does not happen to you. It comes from you. It is a projection of the untrained mind."

Hmm. I never considered that stress can be eliminated entirely. I always thought it was something I had to manage. Admittedly, I haven't been managing it very well, but even if I did get to the gym and use my time more effectively, what good would it really be doing? I would still be on a treadmill to nowhere. I'm not even close to feeling inner peace.

"Is this something you can teach me, Jordan? How to eliminate stress?"

"It's something you can teach yourself, Jack, with the right guidance, of course. And yes, I can offer you some help. It appears you're ready."

"What makes you say that?"

"Humility and an open mind," he says without hesitation. "It often takes a certain amount of suffering before people are ready to challenge the ego and open up to the Truth—and note that I mean truth with a capital T.'"

"So, what's the first step? How do I get started?"

Jordan reminds me of something he taught me as a business leader. He once said that it isn't enough to work hard at something. In fact, this is often what is contributing to elevated stress levels. Instead, we must work smart. We must learn to slow down to move faster and do less to accomplish more. This is counterintuitive and paradoxical, which is precisely why most people don't get it. To accomplish this, we must identify key strategic leverage points—the root causes—so that one change at this level can change everything. This moves our focus away from solving multiple problems inside a box to finding new ways to replace the box entirely. After all, he said, who wants a Six Sigma, near-perfect floppy disk anymore? Improving something that is becoming obsolete doesn't hold up. Transformational change means there is no going back. It is disruptive and innovative and revolutionary.

"Start by identifying the critical root cause to your anxiety and stress, Jack," he says. "Do you remember the Five Whys tool we used in your process improvement events?"

"Yeah, I remember it," I say. "It was pretty interesting."

"Well, that tool isn't just for businesses and project teams. Anyone can use it on any problem they have. Why not use it on finding the root cause to your stress?"

I shake my head in shame. How could I have missed this? The Five Whys is a brilliant problem-solving tool, and I never considered using it on myself or my personal life. What a miss!

I agree to use the root-cause analysis tool on myself and volunteer my wife as my assistant. Judy loves exercises like this, and she has her own stress issues at work. Jordan agrees to meet with me again in a week, and we stand to say good-bye.

"Oh, and one more thing, Jack," he says, shaking my hand and smiling. "Remember that there are twenty-four hours in the day—and it's been that way for a while."

I laugh. "What is that supposed to mean?"

"Think about it," he says. "You said earlier that you often feel like you don't have enough time to do the things you want. Well, guess what? You have the same amount of time in a day that everyone else has. The difference is in how you use it."

3

The Five Whys

The important thing is to not stop questioning.

—**Albert Einstein**

As usual, I return home late from work, and Judy has already had dinner with our daughter Kathleen, who is now hidden away in her bedroom doing homework.

Judy is sitting quietly in the living room watching television and sipping a glass of Chardonnay. Her laptop is open beside her. Evidently, she is multitasking. She greets me from a distance and directs my attention to a meal wrapped in aluminum foil on the kitchen countertop. I glance at the leftovers. Despite a long day at work, I'm not hungry.

I walk into the living room and kiss her on the cheek. "How was your day?" I ask without much thought and even less emotion.

"Typical," she replies without looking at me. "More chaos. More stress. Things never let up at the hospital." Judy works in administration at one of our Boston medical centers.

"Are you making any more progress with your process improvement efforts?" I probe, sitting down next to her.

"The Lean Six Sigma stuff?" she says, pausing the television show she has recorded. "Not really. It's still very mechanical and isolated. We solve one problem, and in the process, we seem to create three more. Our leadership team still views Lean Six Sigma as more of a program than a culture. It isn't anything like what you did at TYPCO. Most people still see it as the next flavor of the month."

"Yeah, Jordan McKay cautioned me about that. He said programs tend to come and go. Culture is here to stay. He even quoted Peter Drucker, who apparently said, 'Culture eats strategy for breakfast.'"

"Ha, that sounds about right. It also reminds me of a quote from Aristotle: 'We are what we repeatedly do. Excellence, then, is not an act but a habit.' I think we're just going through the motions at the hospital."

"Yeah, we use that Aristotle quote at TYPCO now too. It's a nice reminder about process improvement being continuous and habitual, not just an occasional act."

"Well, like I said, our leadership team doesn't seem to get that. It's almost like they're just checking a box that says we're doing Lean Six Sigma. Despite positive intent, a lot of good people are getting discouraged."

"By the way," I interject. "I met with Jordan again this morning. He said to say hi."

Judy sits up and closes her laptop. "What's up with Jordan?"

My wife appears genuinely interested and curious. She has met Jordan several times and finds him intriguing.

"Well, I've asked him for some life coaching," I say. "Obviously, he consults on a lot more than just business and strategy."

"What kind of life coaching?"

I think back to my conversation with Jordan earlier that day. "Mostly stress management, I guess. I want him to help me find more inner peace and balance in my life."

"That would be nice." She presses her fingertips into the hollow between the base of her head and the top of her neck. "I could use some of that myself."

"Well, you know Jordan," I continue. "He has a way of teaching me to teach myself. He doesn't just give me answers. He tests me. He makes me think things through."

"So, what did he suggest?"

"First that I stop thinking in terms of stress management and start thinking in terms of stress elimination—a complete paradigm shift."

Judy sits back, turning her gaze to the ceiling, as if using the blank space to visualize our conversation.

"Then he gave me an exercise to try. He says that stress, fear, anxiety, and doubt are all self-created illusions, just projections of an untrained mind. They're not real, but we think they are."

"Projections?"

"Yeah, projections. He even gave me an example. He said if you're giving a speech to a big group of people and you get nervous, it's because you're assuming something will go wrong. You're projecting a negative assumption."

Judy remains quiet, and I can tell she is concentrating.

"He said you could just as easily project something positive, but people are conditioned to think the worst, especially when we're surrounded by fear and negativity."

"I suppose that makes sense," she says.

"Either way, people are going through life basing a lot of decisions on assumptions rather than facts," I add. "Or we confuse assumptions with facts, and we end up arguing over pure fiction."

PART ONE: THE EGO THOUGHT-SYSTEM

"I see that all the time at work."

"I do too. And many times, we simply don't have any facts. How are we supposed to have facts about the future? This is where faith, courage, intuition, and passion come in. Jordan used the example of a quarterback in football who goes up to the line of scrimmage to execute a play. The quarterback is following a game plan. He has a strategy. He has a play called. The team has been practicing the play all week. But despite all of that, no one is certain about what's going to happen when the ball is snapped. Will we be successful? Will we gain yardage? Will we score? Will we lose yardage? Will someone get hurt? Who knows?"

Judy's lips twitch with bemusement. "Sounds like my day when I get out of bed."

"Exactly," I say. "Anything can happen. So, how do we approach the day? With poise and confidence, like a skilled quarterback and courageous leader? Or with fear and doubt based on negative assumptions and limiting beliefs?"

"So, it's all in the mind," she says softly.

"That's what Jordan says. He said the mind is incredibly powerful, so the more aware we are, the more successful we're likely to be. Can you imagine a quarterback going up to the line of scrimmage with fear? Both teams would sense that like an animal reads fear."

We sit silently for a moment like we often do. Judy and I both like our quiet time. I reach over and hold her hand. She seems lost in thought.

Finally, she turns and looks at me. "So, if I'm feeling anxious and stressed at work, it's my own creation?"

"Apparently so," I whisper, squeezing her hand. "The heart and the gut and the hormonal system respond to whatever the mind is thinking rather than the other way around. When our mind wanders and holds on to ideas that are negative, we feel it in our bodies, even though they aren't real. This explains why some people cry when they watch a tear-jerker movie or get scared when they watch a thriller. It all stems from the mind and what we choose to think, even if it's pure fiction."

Judy's gaze returns to the ceiling. I continue to hold her hand.

"Hmm," she finally says. "But isn't this normal for people? I mean, we all have to be careful about what can go wrong."

"I asked Jordan the same question, and he said it's normal for people who have adopted the ego thought-system. This is a very common way to think, and it's all based on fear and separation and doubt." Again, I watch my wife, looking for a reaction. Honestly, I'm trying to understand this stuff myself.

"So, what's this exercise he suggested?" she asks, turning her gaze back to me. "You mentioned an exercise."

"Yeah, I did. It's a process called the Five Whys. Basically, it's an analysis tool to help uncover root causes, something Jordan calls leverage points. This is essential to leading with knowledge and intelligence. It helps us work smart, not just hard. If we solve problems at the true root cause level, the problem should never return. This is quite different from putting Band-Aids on things or solving one problem and creating several more problems in the process."

"That's exactly what we're doing at the hospital," Judy says. "We haven't found the true root causes to a lot of our problems."

I nod. "Well, that seems to be going on all over the place these days because people aren't digging deep enough to identify the leverage points. So, the Five Whys guides us to five levels of depth in problem-solving. It's relatively simple in practice but profound in application."

"Interesting. Five levels."

"It doesn't have to be exactly five levels every time, but one or two levels of asking why isn't enough. That's where we often end up using Band-Aids or making things worse with side effects. Jordan even gave me an example from a true case. He said, imagine you have migraines, and you go to see a doctor. At the first level or two, you'll probably be prescribed pain medication. This is a Band-Aid. It doesn't eliminate the root cause, and it may even contribute to problems with your liver and kidneys."

"We see that all the time at the hospital. People are suffering from all kinds of side-effects."

"Of course—it's common all through business, healthcare, and government. Now imagine a specialist using the Five Whys. Level one, why are you getting migraines? In this case, the answer is because you're not getting enough oxygen to your brain. Okay, level two, why are you not getting enough oxygen to your brain? Because you have poor circulation in your neck, especially in your capillaries and micro-vessels. Okay, level three, why do you have poor circulation? Because you have inflammation in your neck. Okay, level four, why do you have inflammation? Because you are favoring one side, and your body is trying to compensate. All right, level five, why are you favoring one side? Because your hips and spine are out of alignment. Wow! Really? Your hips are out of alignment? This could be for any number of reasons. Trauma? An accident? Birth defects? But at this level, we may solve the problem very differently. Perhaps you need to see a chiropractor or an acupuncturist, not a pharmacist. Maybe by working on your hips and your spine, your headaches go away permanently, and you experience other positive effects. Jordan refers to this as systems-thinking. It takes cause-and-effect analysis to a whole new level. It connects dots that often seem totally unrelated."

Judy reflects on this. "So, the headaches we have in billing or customer service might be caused by misalignment, so to speak, in operations or dysfunction in engineering. No wonder some of our problems are so hard to solve. We're probably looking in the wrong place for the true root cause."

"Exactly. And anyone who tells a patient with a migraine that the problem is his hips will probably be viewed as a quack. Systems-thinking is not so obvious sometimes."

"So, how are we supposed to use the Five Whys for stress?"

I laugh. "Good question. Jordan didn't tell me how to use it on myself, but he said we can figure it out. We just have to keep an open mind."

"Well, let's do it," Judy says, sitting up and releasing my hand. "Level one. Why are you stressing at work?"

I reflect on the question, landing immediately on Joe and other members of my staff. I then consider the pressure I'm under as president and the insights Jordan gave me earlier in the day. "Well, I suppose it's because I'm projecting fear and negativity, if not consciously, subconsciously. I'm assuming something will go wrong and I will be responsible."

"Like getting nervous before giving a speech," she says. "Okay, next level—why are you assuming the worst?"

"Hmmm, that's a good one. I'm not sure why I do that. It's almost like it's a subconscious habit or something."

Judy gives me time to think. Finally, she asks, "Is it because you don't want to fail?"

"Yeah, I suppose that's accurate. I certainly don't want to screw things up. That's probably why I take on so much work myself. I want to mitigate as much risk as possible."

"Okay, let's take that string of thinking," she says. "There may be other strings where we can go deeper, but for now, let's follow that logic. Why don't you want to screw things up?"

"That sounds funny the way you say it. Why don't I want to screw things up? Because it's embarrassing, and I might get in trouble."

She reaches back to squeeze my hand. "Well, if it helps, I think this applies to me too. And probably a whole lot of other people. I mean, who wants to be embarrassed and get in trouble?"

I think about the club Jordan referenced. "Maybe we're all in the same camp together."

"Maybe," she admits. "Let's go to the next level. Why are you worried about embarrassing yourself or getting in trouble?"

Good question. Why am I worried about screwing up? Some of my biggest mistakes in life turned out to be blessings in disguise. And some of the greatest leaders to ever walk the planet made countless mistakes. What is it about mistakes that I'm afraid of? "I suppose it's because I doubt myself. Maybe deep down I'm afraid I won't be able to recover. And maybe I'm worried about what other people think of me."

"That would explain the fear about humiliation," she says. "I suppose now we could probe two more strings of whys. Why do you worry about what other people think of you? And why are you afraid you won't be able to recover?"

I give this some more thought. "Geez, I hate to admit this, but maybe it's because I feel insecure. I don't really have faith in myself or in anyone else, for that matter."

"Well, it's hard to trust others if you don't trust yourself. And that's probably why you take on so much work yourself, which can obviously feel overwhelming."

I nod, contemplating this analysis. It's almost like I'm running on subconscious programming that was downloaded into my mind as a child. Am I insecure? Do I have a control problem?

Judy pokes me along. "Okay, so why do you feel insecure? Where is that coming from?"

I reflect on what Jordan referred to as the ego thought-system. He said it's a fear-based, dualistic way of thinking. If a person is attached to this way of thinking, this mind-set, they will never feel at peace. They will never feel truly secure. Maybe this is the root cause and the critical leverage point I need to uncover. A change here could shift everything. I think about what life might be like if I felt totally secure and at peace, despite what is going on in the world. Is this even possible?

I shrug. "I suppose my insecurity is coming from my attachment to ego. I just feel this constant need for acceptance and approval and security and control. Maybe this is what Jordan wanted me to identify for myself."

Judy nods. "Well, I think I have the same problem. Maybe we are our own worst enemies. Maybe we're getting in our own way."

Jordan essentially said the same thing. The ego would have us believe the problem is always someone or something else, like Joe, outside of our control. But in truth, how we think and what we think and how we look at things form the basis for everything we feel. Our perception becomes our reality.

4

The Root Cause of All Problems

Forgive them, for they know not what they do.

—**Luke 23:34**

When I arrive at the café, Jordan is sitting in his usual spot, with his usual tea, and looking like he is deep in thought. I find it interesting. In this world of electronics, gadgets, and high-speed connectivity, he seems to have a pace—and a space—all his own.

"Greetings, my friend," he says, standing up and shaking my hand. "What's the good word?"

I sit down and relax, relieved to be out of the Boston traffic. It's only 7:00 AM, and I'm already feeling on edge. "Well, first, Judy says hi. She's hoping we can get together with you and Nicole sometime soon." Nicole is Jordan's wife; when he and I were spending so much time together, we thought it would be nice to include our wives sometimes.

"That works for me. Let me take that back to Nic, and we'll set a date."

"Great." I sigh heavily. "And you'll be happy to know that Judy and I completed the Five Whys exercise, and it seems we both arrived at the same place. How funny is that? The critical leverage point for both of us is subconscious insecurity fueled by the ego thought-system."

"I see," he says without any hint of surprise. There is a sense of knowingness in his eyes. "Of course, that's just the ego doing its job."

I signal to our server for a black coffee. "That's an interesting way to put it," I reply to Jordan as she pours. Jordan talks about the ego thought-system like it's a person. I also sense that he knew we would uncover it as the root cause to our stress. He was just leading us to the answer.

"Well, it's the truth," he says. "Don't take it personally. The ego exists to separate you from your true Source and from your neighbor. Through the eyes of the ego, everything and everyone is individual and separate. This leads to comparison, competition, resentment, analysis, criticism, cynicism, and judgment. We know we are attached to the ego mind-set whenever we feel uneasy or bad. It blocks our well-being, our positive flow. This includes feelings of shame, guilt, apathy, grief, fear, lust, anger, and even pride. This is the club I was referring to when we last met. These are exactly the feelings you described relating to your stress—all driven by the ego mind-set."

I remember all these feelings except pride, so I ask about that. "Yes, pride. Think about it. Pride separates people. It is divisive. My country is better than your country. My school is better than your school. My religion is separate from your religion."

Hmm. I reflect on our last conversation and the metaphor of a hidden club I belong to without knowing it. I suppose pride belongs in there as well. I've always been motivated by a sense of pride and accomplishment. And now I'm almost embarrassed by my physical appearance, which stresses me out even more. "So, how am I supposed to fight the ego?" I ask, eager to free myself from its grip. "It seems like I'll be fighting myself."

That playful glint that I remember seeing often in his blue eyes returns. "I remember thinking the same thing. Stand up and fight! Prepare for battle. You know, I was a very competitive guy in my youth. And then I realized it was the ego mind-set telling me to fight. It was the ego mind-set telling me to stand my ground. Little did I realize at the time that the ground I was defending was the ego's. You see, the ego loves to fight. It loves to create boundaries. It loves drama. In fact, it feeds on drama. It's all about attack and defend and sin and guilt, which is precisely why people feel insecure at the subconscious level. And because the insecurity is subconscious, most people don't even realize it. They have fears and doubts and stresses, but they don't know why. They consider it normal."

"Or they deny it," I interject, reflecting on my own situation.

"That's right. But no one can hide from the truth. It's the truth that eventually sets us free."

I sip my coffee. The rich aroma seems to awaken my brain. "So, how am I supposed to uncover a program or limiting belief if it's subconscious? Wouldn't it be hidden?" Now I feel like I'm preparing to battle a ghost.

"Yes, it is, and that's what makes this transformation so challenging. However, your subconscious thoughts and programs reveal themselves through your tendencies. Therefore, you can start by examining your tendencies. Learn to become more aware of your habitual behavior, your autopilot, so to speak. It can be quite telling."

"So, if I tend to get impatient or nervous or angry, it's because of what I'm thinking—either consciously or subconsciously?"

"That's right. Your attitude, your feelings, and ultimately your behavior all stem from the programs and beliefs you run on, most of which are subconscious. Change your programming, and you change your life."

"Okay," I say. "So, if the ego is my problem, how do I fight it?"

"Be careful, Jack," he says thoughtfully. "Anything you fight, you make stronger. By giving your attention to something, you are calling more of it into your life—vibrationally. Good or bad. This is often referred to as the law of attraction. We manifest what we dwell on. Like energy attracts like energy. Misery loves company. What goes around comes around. Karma. We reap what we sow. You've heard different references to it because the law is universal. Every feeling has an energetic frequency to it, a vibration, so to speak. We can talk more about that later. For now, try this. Put your hand up in the air in front of you." He waits while I do this. He then puts his hand up in the air in front of mine so that the two palms are facing each other. Suddenly, he starts pushing my hand with his. Instinctively, I push back.

"Why are you resisting?" he asks, releasing his hand. "Why did you push back?"

"I don't know," I admit. "I guess it just seemed natural. You pushed, so I pushed."

He nods and rests his arms on the table. "The ego will respond the same way. You try to fight it—it will fight you back. It loves conflict. Ultimately, you will find yourself running in circles."

I think about this. All my life I have tended to want to fight for what I believe in. In many ways, this is what has led to my success in business. I'm just about to say this to Jordan when I stop. My definition of success in business has always been title and position and income. Those I have. But I know Jordan will challenge me on this definition of success because he was in the same place—and yet he wasn't happy. He was consumed with his work. He didn't feel fearless and free. He was stressing just like I am now. How can that be considered success?

He seems to read my mind. "I've told you some of my story," he says. "And I think we share a lot of that in common. When I was younger, I was so attached to the ego thought-system that it was always about more, more, more. It was almost like I was possessed with my work. The ego challenged me to compete and compare. It helped me determine what I wanted and what I didn't want. Clearly, it seemed to serve its purpose for quite a long time." He pauses, as if reflecting on some deep, deep pain. "And then I lost my son in a freak car accident. And then my marriage went to hell, and I nearly lost Nicole. And then my health started deteriorating, and I became a walking time bomb. Despite my best efforts, I had to admit I was not in control. I was not truly happy."

I shake my head, feeling his pain. "Jordan, I'm so sorry."

"That's okay, Jack," he continues. "What doesn't kill us makes us stronger. From the ashes rises the phoenix. I had to learn to let go to let flow."

I've heard Jordan use these words before. To get into the zone in life—the flow, the great Tao, as he sometimes puts it—we must get out of our own way. We must let go of resistance, attachments, illusions, and false idols. We must let go of anything weighing us down because if we don't detach, we live in perpetual fear of losing what we value. This includes people as well as things like jobs and income and assets. It doesn't mean we don't care or we don't love what we have. On the contrary, it means we live with unconditional love and compassion. We care, and we love, and we help, and we support, and we respect people and assets and the planet. We just don't attach our happiness to them.

"Can I ask how old your son was?"

"He was seventeen," Jordan replies. "Just getting started in life. My only child. We did things together but less and less as the years went by. I was always too busy or traveling somewhere, especially as I took on more and more responsibility at work. And even when we were together, I was so preoccupied with my job, I struggled to give him my full attention. I always believed there would be another day."

I nod, thinking of my own children and the distant relationship I have with my dad.

"He was a passenger in a friend's car, and he was the only one who died. Nicole and I were devastated. I wanted to blame the driver of the other vehicle, who ran a red light and sideswiped them. I was even tempted to blame his friend who was driving the car. Couldn't he have been more careful? But none of this would bring our son back. It was a nightmare."

I sit silently. I can think of nothing to say.

"Let's save this discussion for another time. You have questions about the ego thought-system and how to deal with it. I can tell you more about my son later."

Suddenly, I feel very selfish. I can only imagine Jordan's suffering. I search for something to say.

Again, he seems to read my mind. "Just remember this, Jack. Fighting the ego is a losing battle. It's a zero-sum game. You push. It pushes back."

I gather my thoughts. "So, rather than fight the ego mind-set, we simply have to let it go?"

"Yes." A spark of light flashes in his eyes. "But as simple as it sounds, don't think for a minute that it's easy. We're talking about lifelong programming here. Think of it like the operating system on a computer. We can yell and scream all day long at the keyboard or the monitor if we see something we don't like, but if the operating system is full of viruses, it won't matter. We need a whole new operating system. This is not a quick fix. It's an overhaul."

"Kind of like what we had to do at TYPCO to change our culture," I offer, reflecting on the wisdom and depth of our transformation.

"Yes, very much indeed," he says. "We don't fight the ego thought-system and all its self-sabotaging software. We replace it. And to do this, we need spiritual guidance. We cannot solve the ego problem from inside the ego box. Put another way, ignorance is the root cause of every problem on earth. If we go to the fifth level of why on virtually any problem, we will discover that we simply don't know any better. The Buddha said it. Jesus said it. Socrates said it. We don't know what we don't know."

"Is that why I feel insecure? Because I don't know any better?"

"Yes, that's exactly why. You're in a box, and you don't know it. Awakening, then, is about becoming aware of the limitations we're placing on ourselves—both consciously and subconsciously—and letting them go. Here, try this." He takes an index card from his pocket and draws six circles on it. "Take a look at this image and try moving only one circle to end up with two straight lines of four circles each."

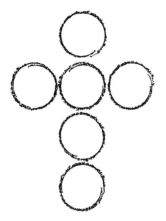

I stare at the image, trying several different options. None of them seem to work. If I move the bottom circle up to the horizontal string, I have four going across but only three going down. After about a minute of silence, I admit I'm stumped.

"Here," Jordan offers. "Let me give you a hint. You may remember this from some of the training we did at TYPCO." He pulls another index card from his pocket and sketches a diagram. "Right now, you're on the top line trying to manage the problem to solve it. You want to be successful. You want positive results, and you're trying your best to achieve them. So, what if I now start giving you motivational speeches and positive reinforcement about your attitude and behavior? Is that going to help?"

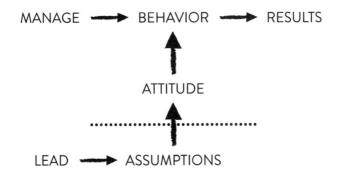

(Perceptions, Interpretations, Memes, Paradigms, Subconscious Programs, and Beliefs)

"No." I laugh. "I'm already motivated to solve the problem. I just don't know how."

"That's right. And you're struggling with the problem because you're in a box and you don't know it. The assumptions you're making and the paradigm you're in are blinding you from the answer. In fact, it may even lead you to conclude the exercise is impossible."

I am listening, but I keep staring at the circles and trying to solve the puzzle. He's right. The problem is not my motivation or intent. It's my ignorance. I don't know how to do it.

"So, my hint is to drill down and challenge the underlying assumptions you're making. Learn to look at things differently. Play with it. Question your interpretation of the rules. Consider what Albert Einstein meant when he said, 'The significant problems we face today cannot be solved at the same level of thinking we were at when we created them.'"

"Yeah, I remember that quote from the training. We have to take responsibility for our problems and learn to think differently."

I continue working on the problem. Jordan sits patiently and watches me.

Finally, he speaks up. "Now, what if I told you the answer is really quite simple."

"I would probably tell you to take a hike." Simple seems relative. Finally, I surrender. "Okay, give me the answer. Let's move on. I get your point."

"Before I give you the answer, let me say this. Most of us go through life trying to manage our behavior at the surface level without ever really drilling down and questioning the underlying assumptions and perceptions driving the way we think. Thus, if we're making decisions with bad data or the absence of valid information, it doesn't really matter how hard we try. We're going to struggle, perhaps even suffer. It becomes an even greater challenge when we're working with others who perceive things differently. Ignorance causes all kinds of problems within teams, and it drives fear throughout the world."

"I hear you." I sigh with surrender. "So, what's the answer?"

He seems to ignore me. "In truth, we have nothing to fear. We are eternal, sacred beings living a temporary human existence.

We existed before we came to earth, and we will continue after we leave. Life is circular, not sequential."

What? Where is this coming from? I've always thought life is a one-shot deal. There are no dress rehearsals. Now Jordan is getting into some deep stuff. Maybe losing his son had something to do with this. I lean back in my chair and fold my arms across my chest. I feel a bit uncomfortable. "Well, I'm not much of a religious or spiritual guy, Jordan. I hardly ever go to church anymore. Is that going to be a problem?"

He smiles patiently, as if knowing something I don't. "Like I said, ignorance is the root cause of all problems, Jack. You are indeed a spiritual being. Everyone is. You just don't know it. Or should I say, you don't remember it."

I am about to argue with him, but I stop. Maybe I don't know what I don't know. Maybe I should shut up and listen. After all, when the student is ready, the teacher will appear. This guy seems to know something I don't.

He continues, "And to be clear, let me suggest a distinction between religion and spirituality. A lot of people confuse the two. Or, they consider them to be the same thing. Religion is generally about someone else's experience and relationship with God. This could be anyone from Abraham to Jesus to the Buddha. Spirituality is about your personal relationship and connection with God. Look closely, and you will see that all the great spiritual leaders said the same thing. They did not teach religion, which is another box defined by the ego. They taught spirituality. They said even the least among us can experience what they experienced."

"Hmm," I ponder. "I guess I never really thought about it that way. Okay, so, now what? How do I let go of the ego mind-set and adopt a new thought-system? How did you do it? And what's the answer to this puzzle?"

He seems to reflect on my question, taking his time with the answer and again ignoring the puzzle. "Well, the first thing I did was ask for help."

I jump right in. "You mean like I did? With you?"

He laughs. "Not quite. Keep in mind, I was at one of the lowest points in my life. I had lost my son. I was separated from my wife. I was overwhelmed with work. And I was my own worst enemy—without knowing it. So, I asked for help from God. And keep in mind, I didn't think of myself as very spiritual or religious either. I just didn't think I had any other reasonable choice. I felt broken. I was essentially surrendering—the ego, that is—and I didn't even know it."

I listen carefully as my friend continues.

"And then a couple of interesting things happened," he says, almost whispering. "First, Nicole asked me to attend a church service with her. Even though we were separated, we both wanted to work things out. We were both in great pain. Now, normally, I considered myself too busy to go to church or give religion much thought, but this time I said yes. Why not? What did I have to lose? So, I went to this service with Nicole. Then, about halfway through the service, the minister started reading from Psalm 23:4. I remember it like it was yesterday. 'Yea, though I walk through the valley of the shadow of death, I will fear no evil: for thou art with me; thy rod and thy staff, they comfort me.' I don't know how and why this happened, but it was as if the minister—and God, for that matter—was speaking directly to me. I was not alone in my sadness and suffering. I had help available to me. All I had to do was let go and let God."

"Wow," I say softly. "From the ashes rises the phoenix."

"That's right," he says. "So, that was the first of two synchronicities, or spiritual coincidences. The second has to do with a book called *A Course in Miracles*. As a self-help junkie throughout most of my career, I was always reading books, listening to audios, attending seminars, and watching videos on global best practices. I wanted to be a thought-leader, so why not listen to highly credible people leading the way? It was like food for my brain. Unfortunately, I wasn't getting much food for my soul. Most of the stuff I was learning had to do with conventional leadership and management practices. There wasn't much on mindfulness and enlightenment outside of New Age stuff, which the management world didn't give much credence to. Anyway, I suddenly started running across references to *A Course in Miracles* from several people I had a lot of respect for. Then, one day, I came home from a road trip, and I was sorting through a pile of mail and there in front of me was an invitation to *A Course in Miracles*, published by the Foundation for Inner Peace. To put it simply, I didn't find *A Course in Miracles*. It found me."

"That's amazing," I say. "Another synchronicity."

"That's right," he confirms. "Later in life I would learn that in Truth, there are no coincidences. Everything happens for a reason, and synchronicities are going on all around us all the time. We just don't typically see them because we're too preoccupied. So, in this case I noticed, and I decided to investigate. I purchased the book. I took the course. And my whole life changed dramatically within one year. You might even say miraculously."

I reflect on Jordan's words, his tone, his humility and his sincerity. Maybe this is the secret to his equanimity and grace. Maybe this is the field of energy he was referring to earlier.

"So, what exactly is *A Course in Miracles*?" I ask. "You said it's a book. Is it that simple? You just read a book?"

"Not exactly. Yes, it's a book. You can also get an audio version of it, and now it's all over YouTube. But it isn't as simple as reading a book. It requires a tremendous commitment. Keep in mind, you are essentially deleting a lot of faulty, subconscious ego programming from your mind and replacing it with miracle-minded guidance from Jesus and the Holy Spirit. Some call this the vision of Christ. It doesn't matter what background or religion you come from. It complements all of them. It teaches you to see things very differently. In fact, I have now repeated the course three times as a refresher, and each time I seem to awaken even more. It is truly a profound and transformational experience. That is, if you finish it. A lot of people drop out within the first week or two. Like I said, it takes a tremendous commitment."

"So, tell me about it," I ask eagerly. "What specifically did you learn?"

Jordan looks at his watch and pushes his chair away from the table. "We will have to save that for another day, my friend. I have another appointment. See what you can learn on your own, and we will get together soon—with Judy and Nic. And pay attention to your tendencies," he adds, setting some money on the table and heading for the door. "They will give you clues about your subconscious programming."

"What about the puzzle?" I repeat. "Aren't you going to show me the answer?"

"In due time," he says, smiling. "See if Judy can figure it out. You'll laugh when you uncover the paradigm you're in." With that, the agent of change vanishes. Once again, he is teaching me to teach myself by getting out of my own way.

PART TWO

I Am Determined to See

We shall not cease from exploration / And the end of all our exploring / Will be to arrive where we started / And know the place for the first time.

—T. S. Eliot

5

Shift Happens

The significant problems we face cannot be solved at the same
level of thinking we were at when we created them.

—popularly attributed to Albert Einstein

When I arrive home that night, Judy is sitting at the kitchen
table helping Kathleen with a homework assignment. Dinner is
on the stove, so fortunately I made it home in time to dine with
my family.

"We were hoping you would make it home in time," Judy says,
getting up from the table. "Thank you."

"Hi, Dad," Kathleen adds, following her mother. "How was
your day?"

I am about to admit to my daughter that my day was long,
demanding, stressful, and a bit chaotic when I stop myself. Is this
a tendency of mine? Do I tend to look at things negatively and
respond in kind? After all, I'm alive. I'm with a great company,
even though the new business unit I'm running is a mess. I'm
home having dinner with my wife and daughter. My son, Kevin,

is doing well at college. In truth, I have a lot to be thankful for. Maybe my glass is half-full.

"Well, it was rather exciting," I reply with a grimace. Judy stops what she is doing and gives me an inquisitive look, her eyebrows raised. "I packed a lot in. How was your day, sweetheart?"

Kathleen looks at me and says somewhat automatically, "My day was stressful."

I exhale through my nose. It's no wonder where Kathleen picked up this half-empty attitude and perspective. She has probably heard her mother and me talk about stress a thousand times. It's common language in our house, which I now realize reflects, like TYPCO does, a culture and the leadership of that culture. I gulp, knowing I am partially responsible for helping my daughter to develop this attitude.

"Kathleen is a little worried about her school paper," Judy offers. "It accounts for a significant percentage of her overall grade."

"Yeah, and writing is not one of my strengths," Kathleen adds with a sigh. "This is by far my toughest teacher and my toughest class. It's the only one I'm not getting an A in."

I look compassionately at my competitive daughter who is apparently suffering from some of the same assumptions and limiting beliefs I have taught her through my example. I didn't even realize it at the time, but I have bitched and moaned about TYPCO for years. No doubt she picked up on it. Is this the subconscious programming Jordan was talking about?

I'm about to give my daughter a pep talk on her paper when I realize that this would be as futile as Jordan giving me a pep talk on the puzzle he gave me. Motivation isn't the problem here. My daughter wants to do well. She is simply struggling with the how.

"Hmm," I reply. "So, you want to do well on this paper, but you're worried you won't get it right. Is that accurate?"

I am now getting curious stares from two different angles, from Judy and Kathleen. Judy's eyebrows are again perched high, and she's giving me that look that says, "What's this all about?" This is not how I normally respond to our daughter. Rather than using a strong, pushy, command-and-control style with authoritative statements and dictates, I am using what Jordan calls a pulling technique. I'm using empathy and thoughtful questions to understand and align with my daughter. To work well as a team, we need to start by getting on the same page. We need to start with the facts.

"Of course I want to do well, Dad," Kathleen says. "I have straight A's except for this class. I just don't know what to write about."

"Well, that was going to be my next question, sweetheart," I say softly, mindful of my tone. "What's the topic of your paper?"

She looks at her mother and then back at me. "We've been going around and around on what to write about for over an hour, but nothing seems to work. I can basically choose whatever topic I want, but it has to be something I feel passionate about, and it has to help people in some way."

I nod, thinking about options. "Interesting assignment. Have you considered music? You love music, especially the orchestra."

She shrugs. "Yeah, Mom and I talked about that, but the teacher also said she expects it to be unique—something no one else is likely to write about. Part of our grade is based on how creative and original it is. I know several people who are planning to write about music and dance."

"I see," I reply, offering a sympathetic smile. "Well, maybe I can help. Let's talk about it at dinner. Meanwhile, maybe you two can help me with a problem."

Kathleen's energy suddenly seems to change to the positive. It's something I've noticed at work too—asking for someone's help, particularly when they are feeling helpless with their own concerns, can help to buoy them. "What problem is that, Dad?"

I grab a piece of paper and quickly draw the six circles Jordan drew earlier. I then repeat the rules and invite my wife and daughter to solve the puzzle. They both look at it carefully, playing with different ideas. Suddenly, Kathleen disappears. Minutes later, she returns with six coins. She lays them out on the table in the same pattern the circles are in on the paper. Next, she starts moving around different coins to find a solution. Judy and I both watch with interest.

Within minutes, Kathleen blurts out, "Aha! I got it!" as she takes the bottom coin and places it on top of the cross-section coin. By doing so, there are four coins in a vertical column and four coins in a horizontal row. I was limiting myself by thinking in terms of a two-dimensional paradigm, which made the solution appear impossible. By shifting to a three-dimensional paradigm, we can see that the solution is simple. I laugh, as Jordan said I probably would when I discovered this shift.

"That's genius, Kathleen," her mother says with a twinkle in her eyes. "How did you figure that out so fast?"

"I don't know," she admits, sheepishly. "I guess I just played with it."

"What I noticed, Kathleen, is that you weren't stressing over it," I offer. "You kept an open mind, and you were willing to explore a variety of alternatives. It almost looked like you were having fun."

"Well, I like puzzles. Maybe that's why I could do it so fast—I wasn't stressed out."

Judy and I grin at each other.

"I guess now all you have to do is apply the same approach to your paper," I suggest. "Let me tell you something. If you approach your paper with the same enthusiasm and ingenuity that you did that puzzle, you'll knock the ball out of the park."

A hint of light flashes through Kathleen's eyes. "I have an idea. I know what I'm going to write about! I can't believe I didn't see this earlier." With that, she grabs her papers and backpack and races out of the kitchen.

"What about dinner?" her mother hollers after her.

"I'll eat later," she replies, her voice fading in the distance. "I want to get going on this paper while the creativity is flowing."

6

A Course in Miracles? Really?

I know of no more encouraging fact than the unquestionable
ability of man to elevate his life by a conscious endeavor.
—**Henry David Thoreau**

I sit down at the kitchen table and laugh. "I think I need a beer."

"I'm on it." Judy chuckles, grabbing a Samuel Adams from the refrigerator and pouring a class of wine for herself. She then sits down next to me and lets out a deep sigh. "What was that all about?"

"What do you mean?" I ask, taking a swig of my brew.

"Well, first of all, your approach," she replies. "That's not how you normally talk to our daughter."

Judy is right. I suppose I live in the paradigm of "father knows best" and "it is my way or the highway." I tend to do the same thing at work. Since I'm the boss, I am supposed to know what is best.

"I guess I'm learning to open up my mind and challenge some of my own preconceived notions," I admit, gazing at the beer in my hand. "It's rather humbling. Besides, truth be told, I couldn't figure out the answer to that puzzle."

Judy looks amused. "Neither could I. Maybe with more time I could, but I suppose a lot of people say that."

"Or use it as an excuse. But time is irrelevant when you're in the wrong box. A paradigm shift sets everything back to zero. It changes the rules entirely."

"So, you met with Jordan again today, didn't you?" she says, sipping her Chardonnay.

"Yes, I did. And before I forget, he's checking with Nicole on dates for us all to get together."

"Great. I really enjoyed meeting them and I want to get to know them better."

"Jordan also gave me another homework assignment. He referenced a book called *A Course in Miracles*. Have you ever heard of it?"

"No," Judy replies. "But it sounds interesting. What is it?"

I think back to my conversation with Jordan. "Well, I don't really know. He suggested we research it and then get together to discuss it. He swears it has completely transformed his life."

"I'm intrigued," Judy says, getting up and grabbing her laptop from the kitchen counter. That computer never seems to be far from her fingertips. Apparently, she was using it for a new dinner recipe tonight. I chuckle. Maybe I should get her a tether for it.

She sits down next to me and begins searching the internet for *A Course in Miracles*. Within minutes, we have scanned several pages of information on *ACIM*, as it is often referenced. We discover that there are three parts to the original publication: a text, a 365-day workbook with one lesson per day for a year, and a teacher's manual. There are also hundreds of articles, videos, and related publications available. I shake my head. Where do we even start?

"It says here that *ACIM* was originally channeled by a psychiatrist at Columbia University named Helen Schucman. It also mentions that this channeling is believed to be directly from Jesus."

My mind wanders to Jordan and his extraordinary sense of inner peace, poise, and grace. This must have something to do with it. He said before his transformation he was just as competitive and driven as me—maybe even more so. Now when I see him, he has a light and an essence about him that is simply hard to describe. Did he learn this from *ACIM*? Did he learn this from Jesus?

Judy continues. "There is also some information here on the Foundation for Inner Peace and the workbook lessons. You can even sign up for daily emails on each lesson."

"Hmm. See if you can find lesson number one. I'd like to get a feel for it."

She nods and starts clicking around. "I was thinking the same thing. What could this possibly be?"

After a short search, Judy finds sample pages from the workbook. As it turns out, each lesson is a relatively short mantra to be recited, contemplated, and practiced throughout the day. I suppose this is the programming, or reprogramming, that Jordan was referencing. He even suggested that for most people, it was easier to go straight to the workbook, rather than begin with the text, because the text is so profound that most people can't get their heads around it. He said it was easier to come back to the text, or reference it, while going through the daily lessons.

"Okay, here is lesson number one," she says. "'Nothing I see means anything.'"

"What?" I question, somewhat alarmed. "What is that supposed to mean?"

"I don't know. It suggests here that throughout the day you take time to stop and look at things and then say out loud, 'That chair does not mean anything. That tree does not mean anything. That car does not mean anything. That person does not mean anything.'"

"That sounds a bit crazy to me," I interrupt, thinking about my Porsche 911 cooling down in the garage. "How can a person or a tree or a car not mean anything?"

She keeps scanning her laptop screen. "Well, it says here to not overthink it. Just follow the lessons and trust the process."

"No wonder Jordan said the course is more than a book. He said it takes a significant commitment to go through the process."

"Well, if it helps, here is lesson two," Judy continues. "'I have given everything I see all the meaning it has for me.'"

I suppose that eases the shock of lesson one a little bit. Maybe by themselves the things I see have no meaning, and I am the one who gives them meaning. A tree might mean one thing to one person and something completely different to someone else. My 911 sure means a lot to me.

"What is lesson number three?" I ask, now even more curious.

Judy clicks through another screen or two. "Here it is. 'I do not understand anything I see.'"

"That's a bit humbling. Sounds like Socrates."

"It looks to me like the original lessons are intended to be humbling—at least to the ego," Judy suggests. "It's almost like everything we've been thinking and seeing with human eyes is skewed, maybe even completely false or misleading."

"That would explain the reprogramming that Jordan was talking about," I add. "He said we have to completely let go of the ego programming to allow the true vision of Christ to flow through us. Otherwise, the ego blocks it with its own set of rules."

"Kind of like that exercise with the coins," my wife says, putting her arm around me and giving me a gentle pat on the back. "We can be blinded by our own assumptions, perceptions, and beliefs."

"Yeah, and no matter how hard we try to make things better inside the box, it doesn't help much if the box itself is the problem."

"Well, what do you think?" Judy asks. "Do you want to take this course with me?"

I think about it. There are a lot of reasons for me to take this course right now, stress being high on the list. There are also several reasons for me to put it off. I'm extremely busy at work. My time is limited. I'm concerned about distractions from work and family. And I don't want to start something I can't finish.

"Here's something interesting," Judy adds. "It says here that the course is not voluntary. Only the time that you take it is voluntary."

"That's bold. It sounds to me like we really have no choice in the long run. Sooner or later, we're going to learn these lessons."

Judy gently massages the back of my neck. "So, what do you say, honey? Will you take this course with me?"

"It sounds like you're pretty determined."

"Yes, I am. Quite honestly, I'm intensely curious. A lot of what I have learned about Jesus through the church seems very biased and skewed. If so many scholars and people interpret this course as a direct communication from Jesus, I want to know what He says!"

I nod in agreement. "That would be the ultimate way to learn inner peace I suppose. Directly from the Teacher Himself."

Judy sits quietly and watches me. She knows I struggle with decisions like this. I have all kinds of excuses to deny or delay *ACIM* right now. She also knows that when I set my mind to something, I commit. I follow through. That's why I don't want to agree to anything I can't complete. I consider that a matter of integrity.

"I don't know, baby. I think I need a little more time to think about this. Can you give me a few days?"

She gets up from the table. "Take all the time you want, honey. I'm going to get started."

7

Creatures of Habit

We are what we repeatedly do.
Excellence, then, is not an act but a habit.
—Will Durant, summarizing a lesson by Aristotle

Back at TYPCO, there never seems to be enough time in the day. Once again, I'm flooded with emails and escalations that shouldn't require my attention. Did I do this? Did I create this dependency syndrome with my command-and-control leadership style? What is everyone so afraid of?

The first email is from Joe going on and on about changes we recently made in customer service. After a minute or two of reading the email, I push myself away from the desk and stand up. Time for a little *gemba*, a Japanese term I remember learning from Jordan. It essentially means get off your butt and go see for yourself what is really going on at the point of action, or crime scene.

Sure enough, I find Joe at his desk, pecking away on the computer. So much for gemba on his part. He looks up at me and invites me into his office to sit down. I remain standing.

"Can we take a walk?" I ask, nodding at the door.

He looks back at the computer and says as if he's very busy, "Ah, yeah, I suppose I can do that. What's up?"

"I want to visit our customer service department. I have a few questions."

"Hmm," he mumbles, standing up. "Are you sure I'm the right one to ask about customer service? What about Mary Jo?"

I turn and head out the door. Why does his answer not surprise me? Here is my guy in charge of leading business transformation, which includes completely rethinking the way we provide service, and he suggests I talk to another manager, notably our customer service manager who barely has her head above water.

I let him catch up. "Maybe Mary Jo can help us, but chances are she's so busy right now trying to solve problems inside the customer service box that she has no idea how to change the box itself."

"The box?" he questions.

"Yeah," I explain, picking up our pace. "The paradigm. The belief that customer service is a bunch of people on telephones all day solving problems that never should have happened."

"Well, we're working on that," he rebuts defensively. "Didn't you see my last report? Mary Jo has developed and launched a whole new training program based on the analysis we did in customer service last year."

He's right. We spent a boatload of money on consultants who advised us to revamp our training program along with our measurement system and incentive program. Now we can handle more calls per rep per day than ever before. From an efficiency standpoint, we made an improvement. At least, that's what Joe and the consultants think.

I stop at the end of the hallway and face Joe. "Why do you suppose our NPS has gotten worse, Joe?" I ask, doing my best to relax.

"You mean since the new training program and incentive system?"

"Yes, exactly. Wouldn't you expect our overall customer service performance to improve after making changes like that?"

"Well, sometimes these things take time to take hold."

I'm about to tear into him with some rather harsh words, when I stop. Is this another tendency? Do I fight fire with fire? Maybe I should try a different approach with him. It seems whenever I push Joe, he pushes right back. It's like that hand-pushing exercise Jordan showed me. Ego fighting ego and loving it. Pure drama. It's just that he's so negative and defensive and critical. It drives me nuts.

Mindfully, I decide to pull with more questions rather than push. "How much time do you think it should take, Joe?" I ask, resuming our walk at a slower pace.

"For a real culture change to take hold? Based on my experience and according to some of the consultants, these things can take five or six years."

I instantly feel my blood pressure rise. I've heard this number before, and I remember Jordan telling me it was nonsense. He said if we believe it will take six years, it will take at least that long, and it will always be perceived as a future destination. The way you change culture is by immediately modeling the desired behaviors with new systems, policies, structures, and methods. It's like Gandhi said, be the change you want to see in the world. Don't plan on it for another day. Or another year. Demonstrate it. Now.

We did this at my former division by pulling together cross-functional teams and running *kaizen* events. Kaizen is a Japanese term for "good change," and a kaizen event is a rapid-improvement event. Within one week, these kaizen teams were redesigning processes to eliminate unnecessary activity and accelerate flow. We would take a hundred-step process down to twenty steps, reducing errors and cycle time and confusion. And then we would kaizen it again a few months later and reduce it to ten steps. In some cases, we eliminated entire processes that were not adding value. And the teams were loving it. They weren't putting suggestions in a box to be responded to months later, if at all. They were taking responsibility for making changes and doing it in real time. We used to say "better, not best," meaning don't worry about making it perfect. Just make it better—fast! It isn't perfect now, and it won't be perfect when we finish the kaizen event. That took a lot of fear and pressure off the teams.

"I expect to see change much sooner than that, Joe," I reply, my voice rising with my blood pressure. "Especially in customer service."

"I agree," he says, now directing blame toward Mary Jo. "I've said the same thing to MJ a dozen times."

"Even though you think it should take six years?" I challenge, my heart now racing and beads of sweat forming on my forehead.

"Well, yeah. And we're already seeing improvements with some of our internal measures. For example, our reps are now on the phones for less time per call, on average, meaning they can handle more calls in a day."

"And how do our customers feel about being on the phone for less time?"

"Good question. Some of them probably love it, if they're getting their problems resolved."

"Do we know that they are?"

"Getting resolution? I'm not sure. We probably have to ask MJ."

"Let me ask you this, Joe. When you wake up in the morning, how likely is it that you want to call a customer service 800-number for any reason?"

He seems to think about this. "Not very likely, I suppose."

"Okay, and when you do call a service number, what do you typically do when you don't get resolution?"

He laughs. "Usually I hang up and call back, hoping to get a different rep. Or I ask to speak to a supervisor."

I raise my eyebrows as if to say, "Of course you do!" "I do the same thing. Do you think this is good customer service?"

"Honestly, I'd rather not call at all," he admits. "The very fact that I'm calling suggests there is a problem with the user experience."

"That's right. Unless the customer is calling to place an order and give us money, we should be asking why they are calling at all. In fact, some top companies today don't want customers calling them for any reason. It's time-consuming and expensive. There are better alternatives."

"I hear ya, Jack," he says. "That's what we're working on now."

"And is that going to take us six years?"

He shrugs. "Hopefully, not six years."

"Let me ask you this," I continue, pressing for facts and data. "How many calls do we get per year, and what are the top three reasons customers are calling us?"

"I don't know exactly. I'm sure MJ does, though. We're supposed to be tracking that in customer service."

"Okay. Tell me this. What is our average cost per call?"

"I don't know. We probably have to ask accounting for that information."

Here we go again. My business transformation leader doesn't know the answers to some of the most important questions about our customer service. We're spending millions of dollars a year answering telephone calls that should not be coming in. I've already done my research, and I have the data. Customers are calling us to ask about their deliveries. Rather than clicking a link to track their orders, we force them to call us. The same thing is true for changing or updating account information. Rather than doing this themselves, they call us. We think that talking nicely to our customers on the phone is good service when our customers don't want to call us at all. More and more of them want easy, seamless self-service. Our NPS confirms that.

Joe and I enter the customer service call center, and there are dozens of reps sitting in cubicles with headsets on. The phones are ringing constantly, and our associates look frantic. We step into a small, private conference room with several telephone headsets that we use for training.

"Let's sit for twenty minutes and listen to some calls," I suggest, putting on a headset. "I think a little gemba might be helpful."

Joe looks at me inquisitively and follows my direction. For the next ten minutes, we hear some frustrating conversations. In most cases, the reps cannot really solve the problem. They can appease the customers but not please them. I'm sure if we used the Five Whys on why we're getting so many calls, we would discover that we aren't doing much proactively to eliminate them. For example, training customer service reps on telephone etiquette doesn't solve a design flaw in our product that causes it to malfunction.

Mary Jo sees us in the conference room and decides to investigate. "Is everything okay?" she asks, stepping into the room and closing the door behind her.

Joe looks at me for a reply.

"Just doing a little gemba, Mary Jo," I say. "I want Joe to hear what your reps are dealing with every day."

"Good," she says. "Sometimes it's absolutely maddening. There's just so much outside our control."

I nod. "Let me ask you this, Mary Jo. How do your reps feel about the new measures and incentives in place to shorten their call time with the customers?"

Mary Jo looks at Joe and then at me. "Do you really want the truth?"

"Absolutely."

She hesitates for a moment as if wondering how to be diplomatic. Finally, she says, "They don't like it at all, Jack. In many cases, they end up upsetting the customer even more because they feel pressured to get them off the phone fast to avoid getting in trouble for missing their quotas. In a way, it's like we are incenting them to anger and frustrate the customer. I've already had three reps quit since we went live with the new system."

Now Joe pipes in, defensively. "Well, you have to admit your team is handling a lot more calls per day than they were before."

"You're right, Joe," she says firmly. "But a lot of those calls are the same customers calling back because they didn't get good service the first time around."

I put my hand up in the air to avoid a dispute. "Look, I think it's time we revisit our whole customer service model. I want to see you two put together a kaizen team, including representatives from engineering, operations, and information technology, to make things better for our customers and our associates immediately. We're not going to wait six years, using hope as a strategy."

"What if the team recommends that we reverse some of our recent decisions?" Mary Jo asks, looking at Joe and then at me.

"So be it," I reply, knowing Joe doesn't agree. "We're not going to defend a lousy system. It makes all of us look stupid."

"I have several reps who will jump at this opportunity immediately. But you're going to have to talk to some of the other department heads. As far as they're concerned, this isn't their problem. They have no idea why the customers are calling us."

"Or how expensive it is," I add, returning a headset to my head. "I'll talk to them today."

Joe sits there like a child who has just been scolded. I might have to start by talking to Joe. Why is he so resistant? What is he so afraid of? And then it hits me. Ignorance. Subconscious ignorance. It's the root cause to all problems. Joe doesn't know what he doesn't know. None of us do. And here I am condemning him with my own ignorance. Maybe instead of firing him like I did Wayne, I need to fire him up like I did Kathleen.

I return my attention to the chatter on the phone, thinking of a quote I like from W. Edwards Deming: "A bad system will beat a good person every time." Again, my blood pressure starts rising. I think we need a miracle in customer service.

PART THREE

There Is Another Way

Success comes to those who become success conscious.
—**Napoleon Hill**

8

What Box?

If we all did the things we are capable of,
we would literally astound ourselves.

—Thomas Edison

Judy has a cold beer waiting for me when I walk into the house. We talked briefly by phone while I was driving home, and she must have sensed I was stressing. Am I that obvious?

I take a swig of beer and proclaim my biggest gripe. "Joe Mulligan is doing his same old song and dance. Sometimes that guy can be so negative."

Judy says nothing.

I continue my rant. There seems to be a continuous flow of blame and negativity and finger-pointing from Joe. Knowing that as president I need to do more than cope with it—I need to change it—seems to stress me out even more. "Today he was getting all worked up about some additional changes we need to make in customer service. It's like he's denying there's anything wrong."

Judy remains quiet. Normally, she jumps in and starts beating the same drum I'm beating.

"Even with data making it crystal clear that we're not easy to do business with, he insists we're working on it." I take another swig of my beer. My wife is now gazing at me with a look of deep compassion in her eyes. She almost looks sad. "Uh-oh," I say. "You've got that look. Out with it."

She walks over and sits down next to me at the kitchen table. "So, he's being negative?"

"Yes," I protest. "And defensive and critical and blaming. It's always someone else's fault."

She frowns. "Like you're doing right now?"

I start to say something and stop. Uh-oh. Did I just get slapped in the face? I prepare to defend myself when I realize that I just accused Joe of being defensive. And here I am going off on Joe for some of the same exact behaviors I use. I'm in the same box he's in: the ego box.

Judy sits quietly and holds my hand, giving me a gentle squeeze. I see the love in her eyes, and I feel the compassion in her heart. Her challenge wasn't meant to be a personal attack. She was just calling me out on something I was too blind to see. I was condemning Joe for some of the very same things I do myself. How hypocritical is that? The ego was blinding me from seeing Joe for who he truly is.

"I guess you're right," I admit, shaming myself. "Thank you for pointing that out."

"You know, honey, a few days ago I probably would have jumped on the negativity bandwagon with you. I understand your struggle."

I take a deep breath and sigh. "Yeah, and apparently I don't even realize how deep it runs."

Judy gives me another squeeze. "Have you given any more thought to taking *A Course in Miracles* with me? It would be nice to do it together. I found an online course."

I'm about to resist a second time when I hesitate. Is this why Judy called me out on being negative, critical, and resistant? Maybe she picked up on this while researching the course. And I did ask her to help me identify some of my subconscious habits and tendencies, like Jordan suggested.

"You're pretty determined to take that course, aren't you?" I say, smiling. Judy is a determined woman. That's one of the things I love most about her.

"Yes, I am. I've already started reading the text, and I plan to start the workbook soon. I'm only waiting to see if you will join me."

Why delay? Maybe Judy is right. Maybe I need to change the way I look at things, including Joe. Maybe I need to step outside my own box and take responsibility for what I think and how I feel.

"What was that second lesson from the course you found the other day?" I ask. "'I give meaning to all that I see'?"

"Yes, that's basically it."

I sip my beer. "So, maybe my issues with Joe have nothing to do with Joe. Maybe I'm projecting some of my own insecurity and fear onto Joe. What a slap in the face."

Judy observes me processing the situation. She knows this is how I'm wired. I need time to think things through. The course said that it is not voluntary. Only the time we take it is voluntary. Maybe I should just bite the bullet and go for it. After all, Jordan swears by it. And I can already see some subtle changes in Judy. She seems more patient and aware than before.

"How much time does it take each day?" I ask.

She smiles, as if knowing I'm about to bite. "From what I understand, it doesn't take much time at all. It just takes attention and awareness throughout the day. The lessons are quite short. You read them in the morning, and then you contemplate them throughout the day."

"I guess I could use some of my commute time," I add, coming up with another reason to commit.

"Sure, why not? I know how the traffic can stress you out. Why not use that time in a more positive way?"

I inhale sharply. "Okay, baby. I'm in. Let's do this."

Judy looks lovingly into my eyes and takes my hand with both of hers. "Thank you, honey. This is a true gift to yourself and to me. I have a really good feeling about this."

I lean over and kiss my wife. "Good. I trust your instincts. Where is Kathleen?"

"Actually, she's upstairs working on her paper. Let me tell you something: that child is determined."

"And to think how stressed and frustrated she was just a few nights ago. What a difference! I wonder if I can do that with Joe."

"It's worth a shot. Wouldn't that be a miracle?"

9

Perception Is Not Reality

Man's mind, stretched to a new idea,
never goes back to its original dimension.

—Oliver Wendall Holmes

Over the next two weeks, Judy and I engage in the course. I find it helpful to have a trusted partner in the process because many of the daily lessons are way outside my box. For example, all my life I've heard the line "Perception is reality." I now realize that nothing could be further from the truth. The earth might appear to be flat when we look at the horizon from a shoreline. After all, humankind assumed the world was flat for thousands of years. Who would have thought it was a giant ball hurling through space at sixty-seven thousand miles per hour and spinning on its axis at one thousand miles per hour? Now we know better. Our perceptions can be very misleading.

The course teaches that there is only one Truth with a capital T. It is universal. It is sacred. And it is not negotiable. There are no individual truths that contradict it or conflict with it. That's what makes it Truth. All or nothing. And when we align with this Truth, with this flow of positive, divine energy and love, we experience miracles. There is a shift in perception, a correction, so to speak.

I also begin to realize during these first two weeks that there is the meaningful, which resides within me, and the meaningless, which resides outside of me. Learning to differentiate the two and then focusing my efforts on the inner work is a critical leverage point. In other words, it isn't Joe who is upsetting me. It's my interpretation of Joe. I am not seeing the "real" Joe. I am seeing an image that I have created through the ego. After all, the ego loves to criticize, judge, compare, and condemn. The Truth is Joe was created in Love by God. He is just as innocent and ignorant as the rest of us. The course teaches me that I am never upset for the reasons I think I am and that I am upset because I see something that is not there. I am projecting my past experiences onto the future. So, when I see an apple and I am asked what it is, I reply that it's an apple because of my experience with apples in the past.

I learn that fear is essentially an illusion. It is self-created when we attach to the ego thought-system, which sees a meaningless world of chaos, sin, and punishment. It is Truth then that sets us free by correcting our minds. Boy, do I need help with this at TYPCO, both individually and organizationally. It's almost like we are paralyzed to make certain decisions and take certain risks because people are so afraid. No one wants to screw up, beginning with me. The problem is that the more we delay and play it safe, the more we fall behind a stream of healthy competitors and fearless innovators.

It's a quiet Sunday afternoon at home. Judy walks into the living room and sits down next to me on the couch. We have both been using the time to rest and contemplate the course lessons.

"What do you think of the course so far?" she asks after a moment of silence.

"Honestly? I'm a bit befuddled. It feels like I've been running on false programming most of my life."

"I feel the same way," she says. "It's like a malfunctioning computer with viruses. The computer is fine. It's just responding to whatever it's being told to do by the operating system and software."

"Exactly. Jordan said essentially the same thing. We really can't blame the keyboard or the monitor because they don't know any better."

"But we do," Judy interjects. "We point fingers and accuse people and defend ourselves and rationalize our behavior without really knowing what is true."

"That's what I'm doing with Joe," I admit, thinking about all the negative things I've thought of him. "And I did the same thing with Wayne at my old division."

"So, do you think the course is helping?"

"Well, that I don't know. So far, it's been a bit confusing and abrupt, almost like it's breaking a wild stallion."

She nods in agreement. "Does it scare you?"

I sigh. "I guess it does. But I think it's the ego it scares. There's something inside me that really connects with the lessons, almost like an ancient spiritual light is being revealed."

"I feel the same way. Maybe that's why Helen Schucman felt so conflicted when she started channeling the words. It makes so much sense when we open our minds, but it's so radically different than how we've been programmed to think."

"Yeah, and that's probably why so many teachings of Jesus have been misunderstood. Maybe some of the people writing, translating, and editing the gospels didn't understand what He was really saying—or meaning."

"And then there are people like us who have our own interpretations," she adds.

"Exactly. Like the meek shall inherit the earth. What's that all about? It's like there's this giant ego-filter screening out the Truth and only accepting ideas that fit inside the ego box."

"Yet all with positive intention," Judy says. "I think most people and all the original scribes have goodness in their hearts."

"I agree. Just like you and I do when we go to work. But that doesn't delete the faulty programming we're running on. It just skews the Truth into something we think makes sense."

Judy holds my hand. "So, do you think these first few weeks of lessons are about deleting faulty programming?"

"Yes, I do. That's essentially what Jordan said it would do."

Judy gets up from the couch. "By the way, have you talked with him lately? I thought we were going to get together soon."

"We are," I confirm. "Let me connect with him this week to lock in a date. Maybe he can shed more light on this course. As of right now, I'm a bit perplexed."

PART FOUR

There Is Nothing to Fear

Blessed are the meek, for they shall inherit the earth.

—Matthew 5:5

10

Dinner with a Mystic

My teaching is like a finger pointing to the moon.
Do not mistake the finger for the moon.

—The Buddha

Judy, Nicole, Jordan, and I sit at a quiet table in a nice Italian restaurant on the north end of Boston. It's the first time we've seen Nicole since Jordan took us sailing over a year ago. The ladies seem to hit it off well, so Jordan and I spend the first ten minutes listening to them catch up on life. Judy shares a few stories about her adventures at the hospital, and Nicole reveals a few insights on her journey as a professor of psychiatry.

At one point, Nicole says to Judy, "So, I hear you're studying *A Course in Miracles*." Obviously, she and Jordan have discussed this.

"Yes, we are," Judy replies, looking over at me and smiling. "We're taking it together. It gives us quite a bit to talk about."

"I'll bet it does," Nicole says.

"Have you taken the course, Nicole?" I ask.

"Oh, yes. Several times."

"Nic is actually the one who introduced me to the course," Jordan says. "In fact, I think it saved us both in many ways. We were at wits' end when we lost our son, John, and the grief was destroying our relationship."

Judy and I glance at each other. The two of us had discussed their loss earlier, wondering if the topic would come up at dinner. I attempt to pivot the conversation. "Did you take the course together?"

"No and yes. I resisted the first time when Nicole asked me. So, she took it on her own. Then, when she asked me a second time, to essentially save our marriage, I went along with it. Talk about ego and resistance. I was clearly my own worst enemy."

That sounds familiar.

"Let me tell you something, Jack," Jordan continues. "The first miracle I experienced by going through the course was a shift in perception toward Nicole. The shame, the guilt, the grief, and the anger I was experiencing at the time was blinding me from the very beauty and grace of my wife. I wanted to fight. I wanted to blame someone. I wanted to take charge. But none of that would bring our son back. It was the first time in my life I ever felt a true loss of control."

"So, you surrendered," I say, remembering a past conversation.

"That's right," he admits without a trace of regret. "As counterintuitive and weak as it may seem, I let go."

A very peaceful silence suddenly shrouds our table. It's almost like someone hit the mute button on the television. People are still bustling about the restaurant, but I hear nothing. No conversations. No clanking of dishware. No background music. Pure stillness—at least, temporarily.

Finally, Judy breaks the silence. "How long did it take for you to get comfortable with the course, Jordan?" I sense she is asking on my behalf.

He laughs. "I'm not sure I ever got comfortable with it the first time around. Keep in mind, I was very attached to ego, and the course lessons are quite threatening to the ego. I believe they are intended to be disruptive."

"It took Jordan a while to fully open up and let go," Nicole adds softly. "But when he did, he became a very different man."

So that's why Jordan swears by this course so much. It was his salvation.

"Nicole, how did you learn about the course?" Judy asks.

The bottle of champagne we ordered arrives at the table, and we pause our conversation to make a toast.

"To inner peace," Jordan offers, raising his glass.

"To inner peace," we all reply in harmony, clinking our glasses.

Nicole waits a moment and then replies to Judy's question. "I learned about *ACIM* from some friends of mine who share a common interest in spirituality. I also heard it referenced by some of my favorite spiritual authors, and I liked how it fit into other practices I was studying—like the Tao and the law of attraction and the teachings of the Buddha."

"The law of attraction?" Judy asks, sipping her champagne.

"Yes," Nicole replies. "It essentially means that whatever vibration we put out into the world, we attract a similar vibration back. You know, like, misery loves company. So, we must be very mindful and aware of the energy we're putting out. Each of these vibrations has an energetic frequency to it that is measurable and manageable. For example, shame attracts more to be shameful of. Grief attracts more to grieve about. Apathy attracts apathy. Fear breeds more fear. Thoughts and feelings of scarcity and lack bring more scarcity and lack into our lives. And all of this is now scientifically measurable."

"Really?" Judy says. "How is that possible?"

Nicole looks at Jordan, who just raises his eyebrows and smiles. "I didn't believe this at first either," he admits bashfully. "But the science is quite compelling."

Nicole continues. "One technique is called applied kinesiology, or muscle testing. I recommend reading Dr. David Hawkins's work for more on that. He developed this amazing tool called the Map of Consciousness, which charts different energetic frequencies like guilt and shame or joy and bliss. Now we can measure the exact frequencies of everything from a song to a person to an animal."

"Dr. David Hawkins," Judy says, pulling out a notepad and writing down the name.

"Yes, and there are some wonderful insights on the law of attraction in a book called *The Secret*," Nicole continues. "You might also want to explore the work of a woman named Esther Hicks. She channels teachings on the law of attraction from an entity called Abraham. She also offers daily meditations on it. You can sign up for them online, and they're delivered via email for free. I get them every day."

I look at Jordan, and he smiles back at me. He seems to know what I'm thinking. His wife, Nicole, has been a pivotal person in his life. She has helped him open his mind to a whole new world, and he is grateful for it. I can see the love and appreciation and gratitude in his eyes when he looks at her. And to think that he almost lost her due to his own egotistical resistance.

"So, you see some parallels between the law of attraction and *ACIM*?" I ask Nicole.

"Yes, I do," she replies. "Once you understand that everything you see, and everything you experience, is a form of energy, you become very mindful of the frequencies you tune in to and emit."

"And omit," Jordan adds. "This is what the course refers to as vigilance."

"Kind of like a radio dial?" Judy asks.

"Exactly," Nicole says. "We have the power to change the channel. We just need to be mindful of the choices we make and take responsibility for our energetic vibration. We can tune in to ego frequencies like grief and guilt or spiritual frequencies like compassion and forgiveness. No one else can do this for us. The course doesn't speak to different energetic frequencies, like David Hawkins does, but it's easy to see the connection. And by the way, David Hawkins is one of the spiritual mystics who references *A Course in Miracles* in his work. He's one of the reasons I finally engaged in the course."

"What do you mean by mystic?" Judy asks.

"A mystic is someone who sees and thinks and lives beyond the ego thought-system. Rather than get caught up in the dualistic way of the ego, the mystic is contemplative, accepting, and forgiving. Perhaps the best example of this is Jesus. Of course, the Buddha was also a mystic, as were many of the prophets and saints."

I think of Jordan. As far as I'm concerned, he's a mystic, and so is Nicole. In fact, it sounds like he learned to live this way from Nicole—and with help from *ACIM*. Maybe I'm destined to do the same thing. Maybe that's why Judy encouraged me to take the course with her. I glance over at my wife and her page of notes. I have a feeling our spiritual adventure is about to get a lot more interesting.

Judy speaks next. "Nicole, you said earlier that David Hawkins was one of the reasons you finally engaged in the course. I'm curious about the word *finally*. Were you resistant at first?"

"And I'm curious about his being just one of the reasons," I add. "Were there other reasons?"

Nicole glances at her husband. Jordan reaches over and holds her hand. "It's a rather long story, but I'll try to keep it short," she says, sitting up straight.

"As a doctor, I'm trained in science. As a professor, I teach science. So, yes, let's just say I was somewhat reluctant to accept things like channelings and synchronicities that couldn't be explained by scientific research. And even though Helen Schucman was a professor of psychology at Columbia and David Hawkins had an MD and a PhD and frequently lectured at universities like Harvard and Oxford, I had my doubts. I was resistant. Nonetheless, I also had a deep-seated curiosity about human nature and suffering. There's so much ancient wisdom that science cannot yet explain."

She exhales slowly. "So, it was more of a diversion at first that I was studying the teachings of Jesus and the Buddha and Lao Tzu and Hafiz and Rumi and Socrates and others. I was simply curious. What did they all have to say about human suffering, conflict, and awakening? What, if anything, could I learn from these teachings? But for me, they were still just words and beliefs without proof. Without science."

Nicole takes another deep breath. "And that's when John died. So suddenly. Without any warning. In the morning, I'm fixing him breakfast and, in the evening, I'm grieving his death." She wipes a tear from her eye. "The loss was shocking."

"I'm so sorry," Judy whispers.

"It's okay," Nicole continues. "It was all meant to be. I just didn't understand this at the time. You see, when John was a little boy, about three, he told Jordan and me that he picked us to be his parents. He said he came to us for a reason."

What? Did I hear that right?

"That's amazing," Judy says softly. "I've heard about stories like this."

Nicole wipes away another tear. "Yes, and it gets better. You see, John also elected at an early age to be an organ donor. So, when he died, his heart was given to another young man in need.

At first, Jordan and I didn't think much about this. We were both so engulfed in grief. Our son was dead."

"And we were angry," Jordan adds.

"Yes, there was definitely some anger and hostility," Nicole says. "Pain can do that to people. Anger is always a second emotion, triggered by something else. We were both agonizing over the loss of our son, and it divided us—at least at the human level. So, we decided to separate and give each other some space. This is when I was again reminded of *A Course in Miracles* by a friend and colleague. So, I took the course. All in. After years of knowing about it and dismissing it, I went all in."

She sighs peacefully and looks at the ceiling, though it seems she is seeing way beyond the carved wood. It appears as if she's giving thanks. "And that's when the skeptic's eyes were opened."

Judy and I look at each other, puzzled.

"You see, that's when the young man who received John's heart came to visit me. He wanted to thank me and give me a message."

I glance back at Judy, and her mouth is now hanging open.

"He said he couldn't put into words the message he was sent to give. He could only explain it with his heart. He then took my hand and placed it on his chest. I closed my eyes, and I felt my son's heart beating, giving life to another human being, to another mother's son. I then opened my eyes, wet with tears, and there was John, appearing to me in this man's body. He looked so at peace, and his message was clear. He said he was alive and well in another realm and that all was good. Fear not. It's time to believe. I gasped and collapsed into his arms, weeping uncontrollably. And when I finally regained my strength and composure, I found myself hugging a stranger—a young man who was now no longer a stranger to me. This gave me all the evidence I would ever need to believe in miracles and a higher power."

11

Misery Loves Company... and So Does Joy

It is not enough to have a good mind;
the main thing is to use it well.

—**René Descartes**

Back at the office, I begin my day by examining the massive to-do list on my desk. Call me old-fashioned, but I still like to write down what I need to do each day, like a checklist. I feel good then when I can check things off the list. Plus, it helps me set goals and establish priorities. The only problem is that there always seems to be an overwhelming amount of action items on the list for the very limited amount of time I have.

I lean back in my chair. Maybe I should learn to delegate more. Jordan teased me about there being only twenty-four hours in a day, and it's been that way for a long time. Maybe time isn't the issue. Maybe I don't have my priorities straight. After all, there always seems to be time to do what I consider most important.

As I sit reflecting on my to-do list, I realize my mind isn't focusing on the present moment. Instead of being in the here and now, my mind is constantly thinking about things I must do in the future or things that have happened in the past. Nicole said this is where a lot of stress and unhealthy feelings come from. And each of these feelings carries an energetic frequency that draws more of that same frequency into my life. We reap what we sow, beginning with the vibrations we put out.

When I think about things in the future and what might go wrong, it brings on fear and stress and anxiety, which attract more fear and stress and anxiety. In other words, I'm subconsciously asking for things I don't want. And when I think about things that upset me in the past, it triggers feelings of guilt and grief and anger, which attract more guilt and grief and anger.

Nicole suggested that the key to inner peace begins with mindfully being present. She said it's how we feel in the eternal now that calls like vibrations into our lives. So, if I can sit quietly and feel good about things, I will attract more good things into my life. She said that appreciation and gratitude calibrate as very positive energies, and this is one of the quickest ways to transcend the ego thought-system. Simply be grateful. The ego doesn't understand these frequencies. It is bound by a "never enough" and "more is better" attitude. To the ego, the grass is always greener somewhere else.

Jordan confirmed that this is very consistent with the teachings of *ACIM*. By learning to take responsibility for what we think, including our assumptions, we are controlling our vibrational frequency. We are influencing the very universe that we live in. We are cocreating with God. Nicole even mentioned a software that measures the vibration we are sending. It's called the EM Wave from a place called the HeartMath Institute. Judy took careful notes on this. Apparently, you load the software on your computer and then you attach a clip to your ear. The clip has a sensor that measures what HeartMath calls heart coherence. Nicole said she would give us a demo sometime if we want. I have to say I'm quite curious. The HeartMath Institute also teaches a meditation practice called the Quick Coherence Technique, which helps us raise our heart coherence—which we can then measure. By using this technique and raising our heart coherence, we are calling more good things into our lives. So, it isn't just misery that loves company. Joy does too!

Again, I stop myself. Here I am, not being present. My mind is jumping from my huge to-do list to my recent dinner with Jordan and Nicole and now to the HeartMath Institute. It's this kind of jumping around that can really affect my heart coherence. I can only imagine what Nicole was feeling when she met the recipient of her son's heart. What a mind-blowing experience. That must have sent her heart coherence through the roof. And here I go again—jumping around. Stay present, Jack. Nicole said the key to raising my vibration to a more positive frequency is to be mindful of positive feelings right now—like gratitude and breathing. Every breath is a blessing. It's a gift. After all, we can't go long without breathing.

Nicole also said that most people don't breathe deeply enough, even when we're not stressed. To raise our heart coherence and put out a more positive vibe, we need to slow down and breathe deeply. She suggested taking six to eight breaths per minute or one full breath every eight to ten seconds—four or five seconds in and four or five seconds out.

I sit at my desk and try it. I let go of my to-do list and the multitude of things on my mind, and I simply relax and calm myself by focusing on my breathing. While doing this, I close my eyes, I place my hand on my heart, and I reflect on the many things I am thankful for, right here and right now.

A few minutes later, there is a tap on my door, and my assistant, Emily, peeks in. "I'm sorry to interrupt, Jack, but Joe Mulligan is here to see you."

I signal her to let him in. "Thanks, Emily."

She steps out of the way. *Oh, Lord, what does Joe want this time?* I realize that this is another negative projection from my mind that has an energetic frequency to it. Maybe I'll try something different with Joe today. If I'm going to assume anything about the future, why not make it positive?

"Hi, Jack," Joe says enthusiastically, walking into my office. "This will only take a minute, and I thought it would be better to talk face-to-face rather than email you."

That's a positive change. My eyebrows rise.

He continues. "MJ and I have pulled together a team to run a kaizen event on our customer service challenges. The week of the event is October 15th through the 19th. We recruited some very talented players, and they are super excited about it. What I need to know from you is can you attend our daily briefings that week, and is there any room to bring in a skilled facilitator? Maybe that consultant you used at your former division? The team could probably use some training and guidance since this is their first real kaizen event."

I sit slightly dumbfounded, leaning back in my chair and staring at him. First, Joe has always seemed threatened by the work we did with Jordan at my former division. In fact, every time I mention Jordan, he starts building up excuses and defenses. Second, Joe has always been very secretive about what he's doing. He has never wanted my involvement or participation.

"You want me to attend the briefings?" I ask, now leaning forward.

"Yes, I do. The scope of this kaizen is big, crossing several departments. We intend to challenge everything: policy, structure, product design, process design, measurement systems, you name it. We may even bring in a customer or two for immediate feedback. Your attention, presence, and support will mean a lot to the team."

I laugh. Is this a miracle? What has gotten into this man? He's acting like a kid on the playground, open-minded and playful. My mind races to Kathleen with her school paper. There has been a shift here, a correction of misperception. This is how *ACIM* defines a miracle.

"You will definitely have my attention, presence, and support, Joe," I reply, standing up and shaking his hand. "You already do."

"Thanks, Jack," he says, gripping my hand a bit too long. "We're going to knock this one out of the park."

He finally releases my hand and turns for the door. I stop him. "Joe, can I ask how this came about so quickly? Honestly, I'm a bit surprised."

He spins around and looks right at me. "Jack, I know we've had our differences, but I took to heart what you said to me the other day. And those phone calls we listened to really got my attention. In fact, it was embarrassing. So, I went back and took another look at our NPS numbers and commentary, along with our costs. I also did some benchmarking. And I don't know. A light just seemed to come on. I think I get where you're coming from now. We need more than improvement. We need innovation. And we need it now!"

12

Time to Meditate

Can you remain unmoving till the right action arises itself?

—**Lao Tzu**

When I return home, Judy is sitting on the couch with her eyes closed, tiny sounds coming from her mouth. I watch her for a minute or two and then can't help but say something.

"What in the world are you doing?" I ask, sitting on a chair across from her.

"It's a Taoist meditation," she says without opening her eyes. "I learned it from Nicole."

I watch her curiously. "How does it work?"

She opens her eyes, which are warm and welcoming. "Well, it's basically a mind-body connection. There are five different sounds, or mantras, that connect with what the Taoists call the five vital organs: the kidneys, the liver, the heart, the spleen, and the lungs. There is also a sixth mantra for the aura, or energy field, around the body. Each of these sounds has a frequency to it that relates well with the vital organs and aura. For example, the sound *ahh* relates well with the heart. So, by taking a deep breath and focusing your mind on a healthy, happy heart and then exhaling with the sound *ahh*, you are calming and nourishing your heart. That's the mind-body connection."

"Really?" I reply, careful not to sound too skeptical. "So, you're using your mind to help your body."

"Yes, exactly. Nicole said that a lot of people struggle with meditation because their minds wander, especially when they're busy or stressed. It jumps all over the place."

"Boy, can I relate to that," I offer, reflecting on my day.

"Anyway," she continues, "this technique allows you to focus your mind on one thing at a time, and that one thing is vital to your health."

"Like your heart," I reply, thinking now about my high blood pressure.

"Yes," she says excitedly. "You should try it. It is very calming, and if you sit very still, you can feel the vibration flowing through your heart. That's what the Tao is all about. It's about flow. It's about aligning with Source Energy, or God, which is all positive, and allowing goodness and peace into your life."

"And this is consistent with what we're learning in the course?"

"Yes, for the most part. Even though *ACIM* teaches us that we're not a body and that the body is neutral, we still have a body to take care of—while we're in human form. And it's consistent with the law of attraction as well. When we release resistance and defensiveness, much of which is subconscious, and we connect with Source Energy, we channel this sacred energy through our bodies to one another. It is all about connecting and harmonizing and getting out of our own way, as you like to put it."

I remember when Jordan told me I needed to get out of my own way. He was very clear about that.

"What are the other sounds?" I ask.

Judy looks at her notes. "Well, the sound for the kidneys is *fwee*. And keep in mind that the kidneys also relate to the brain, the hair, the skin, the ears, the bones, and the hormonal system. So, you want to visualize healthy flow through all these body parts. Also, you want to repeat each sound six times. The Taoists consider this a sacred number."

I wonder how in the world they came up with that.

"The sound for the liver is *sshh*, almost like you are telling someone to calm down or be quiet," she continues. "It's a very calming sound, almost like the ocean surf. And this doesn't just help the liver. It helps the eyes, the skin, the ligaments, the tendons, the intestines, and the immune system."

"*Sshh*," I repeat, visualizing a clean liver. I better remember this one.

"The mantra for the spleen is *whhoo*," she continues. "And it helps with blood flow, immunity, the pancreas, harmony, balance, and overall relationships. It also helps with cash flow," she adds with a grin.

I nod, repeating the sound. Better remember that one too.

"Next are the lungs," Judy says. "Which are obviously vital. And the sound for the lungs is *sss*, kind of like a snake hissing. When you repeat this mantra, it helps to visualize your lungs being power-washed with pure, clean oxygen flowing through your body."

"Ha." I am somewhat amused. "A mind-body power-wash."

"And the last one is *shee*," Judy says. "This mantra is intended to help us relax into God's light, letting go of all resistance, denial, resentment, criticism, and judgment. I have been visualizing my chakras opening and God's light shining through me and illuminating me."

"Interesting stuff," I say, leaning back in my chair. "I'll have to try it." I then proceed to tell Judy about my own meditation earlier in the day and the encounter I had with Joe Mulligan. She doesn't seem surprised at all.

"That's apparently what this is all about. Nicole is very clear on the power of meditation and mind over matter. She even cited several university studies proving the benefits of meditation on the brain and hormonal system. These are just methods to help us become more present and aware. And when we do that, and we let go of illusions and distractions and ego attachment, we flow with more creativity and sacred energy. It's truly profound."

"Yeah, the only problem is the ego thought-system," I reply. "It thinks this is ridiculous."

"Of course it does. It feels threatened by this awareness. It exposes the ego's insanity and delusions. Nicole said this is normal. The ego is defending itself."

"Yeah, well, I can hear it in my head right now, telling me how crazy this is. I can actually feel my attachment to it, with all its fear and doubt and skepticism."

Judy nods. "I can too. It's like a defensive force of resistance. I guess that's the programming we have to delete."

"Well, if you ask me, I think we're on our way to some fascinating experiences. What I witnessed today with Joe was quite a surprise. And to think, a few days ago I wanted to fire the man."

Judy smiles, her eyes now darting back and forth as she gazes into mine. It feels like she can read my soul. Finally, she gets up and speaks. "I guess the first step is to become aware of the ego thought-system and our attachment to it, along with all its drama and conflict."

"That's what Jordan said." I follow her into the kitchen. "He said we don't fight the ego. We recognize it. We can even humor it. And then we detach from it. We let it go."

"Interesting," Judy says, opening the refrigerator. "We don't fight it. We simply dismiss it."

PART FIVE

I Am the Light of the World

Thousands of candles can be lit from a single candle,
and the life of the candle cannot be shortened.
Happiness never decreases by being shared.

—Buddhist teaching

13

Sage Leadership

The sage is always on the side of virtue so everyone around
him prospers. He is always on the side of truth so everything
around him is fulfilled. The path of the sage is called
the Path of Illumination.

—**Lao Tzu**

It is Monday morning, and I'm sitting at the end of a large conference table, preparing for our weekly senior management meeting. This is a routine meeting that my predecessor set up years ago to review our corporate performance, set priorities, and coordinate activities. I have been attending these meetings now for almost a year, and I'm seriously beginning to question their value. It seems to me there is a lot of talk going on but very little action.

One time, while looking for something to do during a long-winded presentation, I calculated how much these meetings cost each year. The number was alarming. By taking the rough salaries of the twelve people attending, and calculating an hourly amount for each person, and then multiplying that amount by the hours we spend in these meetings, I figured we spend well over $150,000 per year to sit here while nothing changes. What a contrast from kaizen, where we don't just talk about change—we make it.

When I first took over as president, I didn't want to rock the boat too much with immediate, abrupt changes directed by me. I wanted to listen to my team and learn as much as I could about this business unit. Now, after observing the amount of wasted time and finger-pointing, I feel something needs to change—fast! We killed a lot of useless meetings at my old division by coming up with better ways to communicate, and people were grateful. Now, I'm tempted to kill this one.

I glance at my watch. It's 9:00 AM, and the meeting is scheduled to start. Unfortunately, we are still missing several key executives. So much for timeliness, discipline, and respect. I sit silently, looking at the empty chairs. There is a buzz of chatter going on in the background by those in attendance, but I'm not listening to that. Instead, I'm feeling my blood pressure rise as we again delay our start. Three people are wasting the time of nine executives.

Suddenly, I decide to try something different. Instead of getting stressed and angry, I will use the time to meditate. I chuckle to myself. Wouldn't it be funny to start chanting mantras using the Taoist technique? That would certainly lighten things up. Instead, I quietly practice the HeartMath Quick Coherence Technique. I begin by focusing on my heart center. I then start taking long, slow breaths to a count of four seconds in and four seconds out, breathing through my heart. Next, I start thinking about things I feel good about, shifting my energy from anger and hostility to appreciation and gratitude. I also reflect on today's *ACIM* lesson: I am determined to see things differently. It only takes a minute or two before I feel much more positive, poised, relaxed, and enthusiastic. I barely notice the increasing number of people now looking at me.

Finally, the last member of my executive team comes in and sits down, apologizing for his tardiness. Normally, I would say something harsh or sarcastic, but this time I say nothing. I simply continue my deep breathing. Soon, all eyes are on me. I glance at my notes and then push them aside.

"Let me start today's meeting with a question." I take another deep breath, like a basketball player preparing to shoot a free throw. "How valuable do you find this meeting?"

There is a long hesitation while my team exchanges curious glances with one another.

"What do you mean, Jack?" one member says. "We've always had this meeting."

I nod. "Yes, I know. We've been doing a lot of things around here for a long time. But that doesn't make it right, especially in this day and age."

No one says a word.

"Scott," I ask our senior vice president of engineering, "how long would you say we've been holding this meeting?"

"I don't know, Jack," he replies. "It's been going on since I got here. At least seven or eight years."

I run another quick calculation in my head. "Okay, so that means we've spent well over a million dollars on this meeting during that period, roughly $150,000 per year. Now tell me, what has really changed or improved because of it?"

Another short silence. Finally, Joe speaks up. "Well, we use it to communicate and coordinate a lot of activity," he says, looking at a few others around the table who start nodding.

"Yes, I'm aware of the meeting's purpose, Joe," I reply, leaning back in my chair. "But what are we really learning? How are we using this time together to lead the company to a whole new level of thinking and performing?"

"What are you getting at?" Scott asks, as if on behalf of every-one else.

"Good question, Scott," I respond, not really knowing what to say. I breathe deeply and then remember a metaphor Jordan shared with me. It gives me hope. "Try this. I want each of you to imagine yourself ten years ago, sitting on your sofa at home and wanting to watch a movie that is not on television." I pause to let the image sink in. "Now, describe the process you use to watch the movie you want to see."

Georgia speaks first. She is our chief human resources officer. "Ten years ago? I suppose I would head to Blockbuster and rent the movie."

"Okay, Georgia. That sounds about right. This was a very com-mon practice back then—and the time between now and then is about the same amount of time we've been holding these meetings."

My team starts looking at one another, as if wondering where I'm going with this example. So, I continue. "And we could map this process, right? The process of going to Blockbuster to get a movie? Beginning with step one, get off the couch?"

A few people laugh. "Sure," Joe says. "We could process map it from start to finish."

"And we could time it, right?"

"Of course," Joe replies, getting excited. "And we could time each step in the process to determine the least efficient steps."

"Sort of like what we've been doing a lot of here at TYPCO. Searching for bottlenecks and constraints and automating systems to move from one step to another step faster."

"We've definitely made a lot of improvements," Joe claims, almost defensively.

"So, how many of the steps in the video process are truly value-added steps?"

"What exactly do you mean by that?" Georgia asks after another moment of silence.

I look at her with empathy. At least eight people at this table have no idea what value-added activity really means, but Georgia is the only one to ask.

"A value-added activity is essentially a task that creates direct value for the capital C Customer, the ultimate end user," I explain. "In simple terms, it translates into what the end user is paying for, meaning that if we do more of it, the customer will pay more for it."

"So, it's doing what the customer *really* wants?" Georgia asks.

"Yes," I reply, "the end-user customer. So, think now about our video example. You're sitting on your couch, and you want to watch a movie that is not on television. What do you really want?"

"To watch the movie," Georgia offers, shrugging. Everyone else just sits there with emotionless expressions.

"When?"

"Right now," she adds. "And without leaving the couch."

A few people crack smiles.

"You mean you don't want to travel to the video store, park your car, browse the shelves, stand in line, check out, and drive home?"

Georgia smiles. "I think I see where you're going with this, Jack. Those are all non-value-added steps. We can come up with all kinds of ways to speed them up and improve the process, but in today's world, the entire process is becoming obsolete."

"And there is no more Blockbuster Video," Joe volunteers.

"That's right," I say. "And that's the basic difference between improvement and innovation. We can certainly make a lot of improvements, but if our processes are full of non-value-added activities like in the video example, we have no choice but to inno-vate. I would say we either innovate or we evaporate."

I glance around the table. Do these people get it? Some of them appear to be so attached to the status quo that any kind of radical thinking makes them feel fearful and uneasy. And this meeting is clearly not adding any value to our customers, as threatening as that might sound to some managers. We sit here week after week with nothing changing in the customers' eyes. I can just imagine the reaction we would get if we sent an invoice to our customers for this meeting.

Joe speaks next. "Your example also exposes organizations that produce videos and supply companies like Blockbuster. They're obviously at risk, as well."

"That's right, Joe," I say. "That's why we need to clearly identify the 'Big C' customers, the ultimate end users, and what they really value. If we don't look far enough downstream in the supply chain, we can get blindsided. And keep in mind, sometimes the end users don't even know what they want until they see it. We have to be prepared to solve problems many customers don't even know they have."

Now several heads start nodding.

"I'll tell you what," I offer, thinking about doing something different to shake things up. "Let's take today's meeting on a field trip." I gather my notes and stand up.

"Where are we going?" Scott asks, following my lead.

"We're going to the main warehouse," I reply, heading for the door. "It's where we are sitting on millions of dollars in cash tied up as inventory that's moving at a snail's pace, if at all. In fact, some of it's been there for over a year." This may be the first time some of the executive team sees the warehouse.

14

The Vision of Christ

The sage is guided by what he feels and not by what he sees.
He lets go of that and chooses this.

—Lao Tzu

I pick up the phone and call Jordan. I'm beginning to experience a significant shift in perception about myself and the people around me, and I need someone to talk to about it. It feels almost like an out-of-body experience, where I'm seeing myself from another perspective. Judy has told me she is experiencing something similar, so I figure I can ask Jordan on behalf of both of us.

He answers the phone after the first ring, and I take a minute or two to update him on what is going on. "So, what do you think?" I ask. "Am I going crazy?"

"It certainly sounds familiar," he replies calmly. "You're beginning to wake up to a higher level of consciousness, and you're starting to see the world very differently, including yourself in the world."

I breathe a sigh of relief. "So, this is normal?"

"Yes, it's normal for people going through this process. It's what the course is designed to do. It's purpose is to help you wake up to a new way of thinking."

"Is there any downside?" I ask a bit nervously.

"Do you mean, is there anything to fear or worry about?" he says after a short pause.

I suddenly get it. "Wait a minute. That question was coming from the ego, wasn't it?"

I can almost see him smiling through the phone. "Yes, it was," he says. "Anytime you're anxious or afraid, it's because you're looking at things through the eyes of the ego, the false self. Your true Self—with a capital S—knows no fear. This is what being in-Spirit, or truly inspired, really means. It means you recognize and remember who you really are and that you are eternal, fearless, and free."

"So, these out-of-body experiences mean that I'm learning to see from a more spiritual perspective?"

"Yes, you're rising above the battlefield to witness life from another viewpoint. Think of this like watching a movie with heroes and villains—a perfect yin-yang harmony and balance—without being trapped in it. The actors are just playing their roles, serving their purposes. After the show, they give each other a hug and go out for a beer. That's how life really is, a perfect balance with contrast. Everyone has a role to play and a purpose to serve, yet we are all connected. We are all One. You see, if we had no contrast and diversity, we wouldn't know anything. How are we supposed to know up without down or light without dark?"

I suddenly think of Rumi's quote about a field beyond right and wrong. "So, everything I observe is basically a lesson revealing itself."

"Exactly," he says. "It's God's Will in motion. We're here to learn. We're here to awaken. We're here for soul development. And the more conscious and aware we become, the more we recognize the beauty and the harmony and the balance in play."

"That's amazing," I reply softly. "And that's what you mean by flow, right?"

"Yes, flow is always happening, even when we don't see it. It's energy in motion, and God is Source Energy. God is also all good and all positive. There is no source of evil or bad, despite what many people think. There is only resistance to that which is good. True love has no opposite."

"So, that's what you mean by people getting in their own way. It's the ego attachment that blinds us from the positive flow of energy and well-being."

"That's correct. The ego is like the news, always pointing out what's wrong with the world."

"And when we get into that negative or angry vibe, we're simply asking for more trouble," I interject.

"Yes. And it's even more powerful when we think this way collectively."

"Because it puts the entire world at risk, right? When whole populations are afraid, negative, and angry, we're asking for disaster."

"Yes, and God, or universal energy, always delivers," he says. "That's why *ACIM* reminds us that we're all ministers of God, here to find and teach salvation. It's the secret to world peace: beginning with inner peace. We're all one with God and in God, even if the ego sees us as separate. This is what Jesus is saying, that even the least among us can do far greater than He did."

I contemplate what Jordan is saying. So, enlightenment isn't a goal or a destination we reach. It's a matter of recognizing our own divinity and eternal nature. It's a "letting go and waking up" process.

"Does it ever frighten you when you have an out-of-body experience?" I ask, returning to my own discomfort with it.

"You know the answer to that, Jack," Jordan replies. "It frightens the ego because the ego would have you believe you are an individual body, finite with a birth and a death, and separate from God."

"So, when I step outside my ego programming and attachment and I see the world with the vision of Christ, this shift is an example of a miracle?"

"That's one example. A miracle is any shift in perception that corrects misperception. It reveals Truth over falsehood. It reconnects you with your true Self."

"Hmm. Then I think I'm already experiencing some corrections. Do you remember me telling you about Joe Mulligan, our vice president of business transformation?"

"Yeah, I remember," Jordan says. "You were pretty frustrated with the guy. You even thought you might have to let him go."

"That's right," I say. "The guy was basically driving me nuts."

"And now?"

"Now I see him totally differently. He wasn't driving me nuts. I was driving me nuts. I wasn't seeing him as a son of God through the vision of Christ. I was seeing him as an ego through my own ego. It was like we were in an ego battle, feeding on the drama. Kind of like that movie metaphor you just used."

"Yes, the ego loves drama."

"And now by seeing him differently, he is seeing me differently," I add. "He even asked about getting your help with an upcoming kaizen event."

"Really?" Jordan says. "That's an about-face."

"You bet it is. I told him I would ask you about it."

"Well, you know I'm willing to help in any way I can. Just say the word."

PART SIX

Love Holds
No Grievances

As you sow, so shall you reap.

—**Proverb**

15

No More Complaints

*Never doubt that a small group of thoughtful, committed people
can change the world. Indeed, it is the only thing that ever has.*

—Margaret Mead

When I return home, I find Judy and Kathleen huddled around
the kitchen table. Kathleen is grinning from ear to ear.

"Guess what, Dad?" she shouts enthusiastically. "I got an A on
my paper!"

Judy looks over at me lovingly. "And you should read this," she
says, gently patting our daughter on the back. "It's brilliant."

"Well, I'm not surprised," I say, dropping my briefcase on a
kitchen chair. "We have a brilliant daughter. I'd love to read your
paper, sweetheart."

She hands me the paper, and I glance at the title: "The Dangers
of Stress and What You Can Do About It."

"Very timely and very important," I say.

"That's the whole idea, Dad," she boasts. "And I think that's
why I got an A. This is a paper that can help people everywhere.

Who can't relate to stress? It explains the dangers of stress, mentally, physically, emotionally, and socially, and it reminds people that stress is self-created. So, since we create it, we're the only ones who can do anything about it."

"Hmm," I reply. "It sounds like you really did your homework."

"I did, Dad. And I used the tips on myself while I wrote the paper. It really worked. I didn't feel stressed at all. In fact, I felt excited."

Let go and let flow, I think to myself with a smile. Is this another synchronicity? "Well, congratulations, sweetheart. I knew you had it in you."

With that, my daughter gives me a hug and races out of the room. Judy looks like a weight has been lifted from her shoulders. Shift happens.

Later that night, Judy and I sit down and turn on the evening news. This has been a customary practice of ours since early in our relationship. We were both raised by news junkies, and we were both programmed to think that we always had to know whatever the talking heads told us. We had to be in the know. It also gave us something to debate even though we had no real control over the issues we were debating.

Within ten minutes, we hear about a murder, a car crash, a devasting forest fire out West, the opioid crisis, and two drug commercials with a string of dangerous side effects.

"I don't know, baby, but I'm not liking this news vibe much these days," I finally say. "How about we put on some music instead? Or maybe a comedy?"

"Funny you should say that, honey. I was just thinking the same thing." She grabs the remote and clicks to a classical music channel. Andrea Bocelli's voice fills the room.

I immediately feel a difference. Wow, I wonder what this music calibrates at energetically? We sit quietly for a minute or two listening to the powerful voice of this brilliant Italian singer. He's singing "Can't Help Falling in Love." Instinctively, I reach for Judy's hand and give her a gentle squeeze. She turns toward me, her hazel eyes dancing in the light.

"You know," I say, "with everything we're learning about energy and frequencies and the law of attraction, I would hate to think we're drawing negativity into our lives by tuning into some of the miserable stuff on TV."

She says, "I agree. But we probably are. This might be some of that subconscious programming we were talking about earlier. Maybe we've been downloading fear and paranoia and hostility into our lives without even knowing it."

I think about my antagonistic relationship with Joe and other members of my staff. And then I think about the challenges I face within my own family, beginning with my dad. "Yeah, and these tendencies might reveal some more thoughts we need to delete— like, I *think* I need to know this stuff."

"Or the whole thought-system," Judy adds. "It seems to me that most of these news stories just feed the ego. Maybe that's why we're now questioning the value of it. We used to have a common vibe with the news, a hunger for it. Now, we find it disturbing and distasteful. Something has shifted."

"Yeah, Jordan told me that would happen. He said it wouldn't just be things like television and music, though. It would be people too. Including family and friends."

"Hmm," she says. "Family and friends?"

"Yeah. Remember, the law of attraction says that like energies draw like energies. So, negativity is going to draw negativity. If we suddenly start focusing on positivity, what do you think will happen with some of our negative friends and family? How do you think they will feel when they are around us?"

"Interesting," she says. "And I guess that works both ways. Negative people may find us annoying while positive people who we found annoying before may reconnect."

I think again about my mother and father and brother and sister. I'm the oldest of three children, and we've had a very distant relationship since I moved away for college many years ago. Before that, my brother and I got along all right, but we were both very competitive, and it often resulted in abuse. Let me put it this way. We fought a lot. We both had to win. My sister was different. She was competitive but in a quieter way. We love each other but in a more "tough love" kind of way. The same is true with my dad. He has *tough love* written across his forehead. He raised us to work hard and fight for what we want. My mom was quieter and more compassionate. And there is no doubt she played second fiddle to my father.

I also think about some very positive people I've met over my lifetime who seemed to distance themselves from me. Is it because I was so driven, competitive, and tough they just didn't like being around me? Is this what caused a change in my relationship with Joe? By shifting my focus and vibe, did he feel a difference? My staff seems to react differently to me now too, ever since I started taking the course. By letting go of my attachment to ego, it seems more positive flow is revealing itself through the people I am closest to.

"It's funny," I say. "It seems like a lot of people are seeking peace in the world, but they're not at peace with themselves. It's like thinking that someday I can be at peace when the rest of the world stops fighting."

Judy nods. "That could be a long time. The world has been fighting wars for thousands of years. Do you really think it's going to stop anytime soon?"

"So, the key is to find inner peace in any situation," I offer, thinking aloud. "To rise above the battlefield and see things differently. World peace begins with each one of us, internally."

"How about this idea?" Judy says, moving closer to me on the couch. "How about we both commit to letting go of grievances and complaints? No more negativity. Life now is all about joy and appreciation and gratitude."

"Let's try it," I reply, kissing my wife softly on the lips.

She kisses me back. She doesn't tell me that this is one of the tips in Kathleen's paper. I trust she wants me to discover this for myself when I read it.

We sit quietly for a moment, enjoying the music. Another Andrea Bocelli song comes on. This one is called "The Prayer," and it features Celine Dion. As I listen to the words, I almost feel like crying. Another synchronicity? I don't know. But now I feel compelled to dance. I grab Judy's hand and pull her gently from the couch. It's time to make our own news.

16

Easier Said Than Done

The field is the sole governing agency of the particle.

—**Albert Einstein**

Back at work, I can't help but witness a culture of fear, doubt, uncertainty, and stress. We're making improvements, but it's becoming more and more clear to me that the negative vibe we share collectively is restricting us from true innovation and growth. It's like that exercise with the coins. The answer is relatively simple to someone who is truly open-minded, playful, and creative, but we can't see it. Our culture, or field of energy, is holding us back.

My purpose now is clear. I must find ways to change the field, the vibration we all share. In retrospect, this is what I did with my former division. I just didn't think of it this way. Jordan obviously did. He didn't use these words or explain it in this way, but he demonstrated it. He was very subtle in guiding me. I suppose if he were to start talking about miracle-minded management too early in the process, he would lose me. My state of mind wouldn't take him seriously. Instead, he challenged me to change the way we do things, which carries a vibration, by changing the way we do things. He said culture is essentially synonymous with systems and structures. Therefore, by using kaizen events to rapidly change the systems and structures we were using, including policy, design, process management, control systems, hiring, training, measurement, and incentive, we would be changing our culture. We would be changing our vibration.

Jordan also taught me that the methodology we use to make these changes is critically important. Rather than using a tired, old, "meet every week and talk about it" approach, we used targeted kaizen events to get the job done quickly and with the people who are closest to the process. This change, in and of itself, sent a very powerful message to our associates. We aren't doing change *to* you. We are doing it *with* you!

When I first witnessed how Jordan trained our associates and facilitated these kaizen events, I used to wonder what magic water he was giving them. It was quite miraculous to watch. Prior to the event, and even early in the week during the event, a lot of people were anxious, skeptical, and nervous. *Is this for real?* they probably wondered. What if we screw up? Yet Jordan expressed no doubt. He had complete faith in himself and in the team and in the process. Apparently, his energy was contagious. Now I know his secret. He was using miracle-minded management to influence the collective energy of the group. He didn't call it this, of course. But it seems to fit. He was approaching work with a different mind-set, a correcting mind-set, a miracle mind-set.

Unfortunately, my current senior management team and our associates in this business unit never experienced these kaizen events. My former division was isolated, and I went outside of corporate protocol to lead the changes. You might say that despite my own fear and insecurity, I took a risk. I had to. Our division was a dinosaur on the road to extinction.

So, maybe the best approach for me now is the same approach I used with Jordan. We define targeted areas for innovation and improvement. We pull cross-functional teams together to collect facts and data on our current process—including the good, the bad, and the ugly. We train these teams on effective data-gathering and analysis techniques. The teams then do a thorough cause-and-effect analysis of why we have the problems we have. This leads us to strategic leverage points, or what I like to call the root-root causes. It's at this level we can make truly sustainable change. By getting to the key leverage points, one change can eliminate multiple undesirable effects. I remember Jordan asking me, would I rather have one or two projects that solve significant issues or twenty projects that only get at symptoms?

My role in this is to deploy the new "way," or culture, by focusing my leadership team on top priorities and making sure we are all aligned and united. We can do this by commissioning high-performance teams to gather facts and data across value streams and point out where we are dysfunctional. Of course, this also helps align the project teams, eliminating a lot of the confusion and functional finger-pointing we have now.

The more I think about our new roadmap, the more I get excited. Nicole said that this is a good sign. She referred to it as our emotional guidance system—from Esther Hicks's channeling of Abraham and the law of attraction. Apparently, whatever we're feeling is telling us something about our vibration and our alignment with flow. If we're feeling excited and enthusiastic, it means we're getting out of our own way and allowing Source Energy to flow through us. On the other hand, if we're feeling anxious and afraid, worried or stressed, we're not aligned with flow. Our thinking and resistance are blocking well-being. So, all this time when I've been coming to work feeling doubtful and negative, I've been making things worse—subconsciously. Instead of leading with miracle-minded management, I was leading with the fear-based, dualistic ego. I was influencing our culture in a very negative way. What a revelation!

I think back to the simple transformation I witnessed with my daughter and her paper. In a matter of minutes, Kathleen went from a negative, doubtful, anxious mind-set to one of excitement, exhilaration, and joy. Even though she was still the same person, with the same writing skills, facing a daunting challenge, her energy shifted as soon as her mind-set shifted. Could it be that simple? *ACIM* teaches there is no order of difficulty to miracles. It's the same process—one of forgiveness, letting go, and correction—coming from the same source of energy. Maybe this explains why Jesus always asked, do you believe? Most of us probably don't.

I open my briefcase and pull out my daughter's paper. I wonder what else I can learn from this gifted kid. Her opening line makes me grin. *Got stress? Delete it!*

PART SEVEN

I Am Entitled to Miracles

The one in whom no longer exist the craving and thirst
that perpetuate becoming; how could you track that
Awakened One, trackless and of limitless range.
—**The Buddha**

17

Hidden Teachers

What is this precious love and laughter budding in our hearts?
It is the glorious sound of a soul waking up.

—**Hafiz**

On my way home from work, I find myself in another major traffic jam. Horns are honking, lights are flashing, and people are cutting each other off for no apparent reason. Who screwed things up this time? What a mess! It seems day after day there is some issue blocking flow. Typically, it takes me about an hour to get home. Tonight, it will probably take two. It doesn't matter how fast my 911 is. I'm part of a system with constraints. I shake my head in disgust. Another hour away from my family. Another reminder of my challenges at TYPCO.

I'm about to join the crowd with frustration and anger when I remember my commitment with Judy. We promised to be positive. No more grievances and no more complaints. Ouch! How am I supposed to enjoy a traffic jam? This is easier said than done. I really feel like screaming at someone and laying on the horn. No wonder my blood pressure is so high. This is a complete waste of time, and I want to get home.

I reflect on some of the lessons I'm learning from *ACIM*. Inner peace, like heaven, isn't a destination. It's a state of mind—anywhere and anytime and always available to us. It's moments like these that simply test us. They give us a chance to practice. In fact, some of our greatest teachers are our greatest adversaries. We learn patience from people who test our patience. A soul mate isn't limited to a single, romantic relationship with a lover. It's an agreement we have with other souls to help us advance one another. Perhaps the best example of this is Jesus and Judas. Everyone wants to condemn Judas, but Jesus picked Judas as a very close friend to do exactly what he did. This was a soul contract. It was meant to be.

Maybe I'm supposed to learn something from this traffic. Maybe this is one of those yin-yang moments that is intended to teach me a valuable lesson. *ACIM* says every lesson is a miracle. I inhale again. As I reflect on the situation, it reminds me a lot of the noise and chatter and dysfunction going on at TYPCO. People are all lobbying for position and competing to get ahead. Like this overcrowded highway system, our work systems are set up similarly, I suppose. Our associates are just doing whatever they can to cope with the confusion and do the best they can.

My conscious mind continues to wander, racing from the past to the future without much attention on the present. Meanwhile, my subconscious mind, which has no choice but to be present, monitors my surroundings, drives the car, regulates my blood pressure, and does a thousand other things. I remember Jordan telling me that our subconscious mind, or our habitual mind, essentially governs our daily lives over 95 percent of the time because our conscious mind is too busy focusing on another time and place.

I remember an audio program Jordan loaned me. He said he found it very enlightening. It's a program from cell biologist Bruce Lipton called *The Wisdom of the Cells*, and it speaks to this very phenomenon. The mind has extraordinary power and influence. Maybe I should listen to it and pay attention. It's been sitting here in my car console for months. Come to think of it, I'm not even aware the radio is playing right now. All I hear is traffic.

I retrieve the audio program from my console and begin playing it. If I'm going to sit here in traffic, I might as well try something positive and productive. Forty minutes later, I pull into my driveway, and it appears only minutes have gone by. In fact, I find myself wanting to stay in the car longer to finish listening to what Dr. Lipton has to say about the subconscious mind and the biology of belief. He claims the subconscious mind is approximately one million times more powerful in processing data than the conscious mind. That's amazing. No wonder it runs most of our lives. But he also says it is not capable of creativity. It only replays whatever has been downloaded into it from the past. It is our autopilot, so to speak. Therefore, if we are to successfully change habits and sustain the change, we must reprogram the subconscious mind. Nothing else will work in the long run. The conscious mind can be as creative and willful as possible, but the subconscious mind runs on experience, all of which comes from the past.

I relate these insights to my challenge of being more positive, confident, and stress-free. My autopilot response, or habitual tendency, is to find fault when things go wrong, like the traffic jam. The same is true at TYPCO. I jump to conclusions. I pass judgment. I look for people who are at fault. I get angry. It feels almost instinctive. And then my blood pressure rises, and I get defensive. These are some of my most common tendencies, all buried in my subconscious mind. I suppose at this point it doesn't really matter where the programming came from. I could blame my dad or my upbringing as a child, but that doesn't change anything. The only thing that ultimately changes my response is my deletion of this old, negative, fear-based programming. Like Jordan said, I need to let go to let flow.

As I turn off the car and head into the house, I reflect on how quickly we can change our vibration by changing our attention. Kathleen did it with her paper. Judy and I did it with some music. I just did it with the traffic. Of course, it helps to have a little guidance from someone. I helped Kathleen think differently. Andrea Bocelli brought peace into our home with his music. Bruce Lipton helped me think differently. And in all these cases, we had a negative perception about something that was self-generated. Getting defensive and blaming others doesn't change anything. We need to take responsibility for changing the channel ourselves. The old saying "Seek and ye shall find" is true whether we seek positive or negative. Both are always there for us to see. It's our choice to decide what to focus on.

18

Miracle-Minded Management

It is one of the most beautiful compensations of this life that no man can sincerely try to help another without helping himself.

—Ralph Waldo Emerson

I'm a bit surprised when I first arrive at Jordan and Nicole's condominium in downtown Boston, near the Commons. He and Nicole invited Judy and me to attend an ACIM gathering at their home, a place we've never been. Despite knowing this man for several years now, I didn't know what to expect. On the one hand, they can probably afford anything they want. On the other hand, they don't appear to want much. Their condo is relatively small, contemporary, and very Zen-like. It's surrounded by beautiful gardens, small fountains, and extraordinary art. I immediately feel calm and welcome. Inside the condo are Italian tile floors, modern furniture, tropical plants, salt rocks, scented candles, and warm lighting. Again, I feel an instant sense of equanimity and peace. Evidently, Judy feels the same way. I observe her taking it all in with a warm smile on her face.

"What's that scent?" Judy asks Nicole as we enter the living room, which is quietly buzzing with the conversation of about half a dozen other guests sitting in a circle. "It smells amazing."

"Oh, that's frankincense," Nicole replies, pointing out an essential oil diffusor on the piano. "It's a very healthy oil."

"No wonder the Magi brought it to Jesus as a gift." I smile.

"Yes, I think the Magi knew what they were doing. Frankincense and myrrh have been used for thousands of years as healing agents."

"And some believe the gold to be turmeric, because of its color, and it has healing properties," Jordan adds, walking into the room. "After all, what would Jesus need with actual gold?"

Judy and I look at each other. She winks, amused. "Makes sense to me," she says. "I just never thought of it that way."

"Let me introduce you to our other guests," Jordan continues. "This is Adam, Sheila, Tony, Erica, and Lilly. We've been meeting together to discuss *ACIM* for about two years now, and we all find it quite enlightening. Friends, this is Jack and Judy."

We greet the other guests and then join the circle. Jordan proceeds to serve sparkling water, champagne, or wine to most of the attendees, including Nicole and himself. He grabs a Samuel Adams from the fridge for me. An assortment of cheeses, crackers, nuts, and vegetables are on the coffee table in front of us.

Jordan takes his place on an Eames chair in the circle and nods to Nicole. She then opens the meeting, simply and eloquently. "Greetings, everyone. How about we begin tonight by sharing a short personal story relating to *ACIM*? I trust Jack and Judy will find this helpful and may even have a story of their own to share."

My mind immediately races to my experience with Joe. Then Kathleen comes to mind. Suddenly, I stop. Someone is talking, and I'm not listening. *Be present, Jack. Be present.*

"At the time, I was going through a very painful divorce," Adam is saying. "After twenty-six years of marriage and four children together, my wife decided she wanted something else. And someone else. It was devastating." He looks at Sheila. "So, a friend of mine suggested *ACIM*, and I figured, what do I have to lose? I felt broken, lost, and alone. I also felt betrayed. How could my wife do this to me? And to the kids? Yet the more hostile and condemning I became, the more imprisoned I became. That's when I learned the true meaning of forgiveness. The course taught me that. I had to learn to forgive—not from an ego perspective, where I'm right and you're wrong, but I still forgive you. That was a real shift for me. I had to completely let go of the ego way of thinking. This is true forgiveness. And when I did that, I felt free. I was no longer carrying this heavy emotional baggage with me. I learned to see my ex-wife in new light, hoping and praying for the best for her."

That's an entirely different level of forgiveness. There is no right and wrong duality. There is simply acceptance and faith in a higher will. Forgive them for they know not what they do.

Sheila speaks next. "My situation was similar, yet different."

"By the way," Adam interrupts, resting his hand on Sheila's forearm. "Sheila is the friend who introduced me to *ACIM*, and I thank God every day for this miracle."

"God works in mysterious ways." Then Sheila's expression shifts as she grows wistful. "I lost my husband several years ago to cancer, and I was riddled with guilt for not knowing more about how to release and prevent this common disease."

That's an interesting way to put it, I think to myself. Release and prevent?

"You see, I was a physician's assistant at the time, trained in conventional, allopathic medicine. I had no training in diet and nutrition and high-alkaline foods that reduce the risk of cancer. And I had no knowledge of treatments like hyperbaric oxygenation chambers. So, when my husband became ill, we followed the standard protocol with poisons and radiation. Instead of using mindful, holistic practices and techniques to let the cancer go, we focused on it. We dwelled on it. We feared it. We became consumed by it. And it seems like the more we fought it, the more it fought back."

Just like the ego, I recall Jordan saying. Whatever we fight, we make stronger.

"Anyway, he eventually died from the chemotherapy, and I somehow blamed myself." Sheila wipes a tear from her eye. "Little did I know that I was imprisoning myself with these thoughts and feelings of shame, guilt, and grief. That's when Nicole introduced me to *ACIM* and, like Adam, I figured I had nothing to lose. So, I took the course, and it changed my life. Now I teach it and offer it to anyone who is ready. I also attend holistic health conferences around the country where I'm learning all kinds of helpful tips on mind-body wellness."

"Mind-body wellness," I repeat. "That sounds like an interesting topic to explore."

"Well, we can save some of the details on that for another day," Sheila replies. "But let me just say this. Mindfulness, meditation, and *ACIM* are a great place to start."

Adam urges, "Tell them about the woman you met at that health conference in Los Angeles. This is really cool," he says to all of us.

Sheila looks at Nicole, who smiles. "Sure," Sheila says. "I met this woman who was diagnosed with terminal pancreatic cancer six years prior. She was given a few weeks to live, after rounds and rounds of chemo and radiation. So, she went home to die. Then a friend told her about this wellness center in West Palm Beach,

Florida, called Hippocrates. She figured she had nothing to lose, so she went. A few months later, her cancer was completely gone. It simply left her body. It couldn't survive there because of the changes she was making. Now, many years later, she is as fit and healthy as she ever was."

The other guests murmur, "Wow," or, "I never heard that story."

Sheila blushes. "Yeah, well, I know it's hard to believe for some people, but Hippocrates has lots of cases like that. This just fueled my hunger for more knowledge on alternative health practices—like diet, nutrition, yoga, and meditation."

"And Earthing," Adam volunteers enthusiastically. "Sheila learned about this simple practice called Earthing, or grounding. It's when you touch the earth with your skin. Your body gets flooded with electrons from the earth—which neutralize free radicals in your body. This improves your circulation, reduces inflammation, and even helps you sleep better."

I look at Jordan.

He reads my skepticism and calls me out. "Check it out, Jack. The science on Earthing is quite compelling. Nic and I have been doing it for years. We use grounded bedsheets now, which makes it easy, especially in the winter."

I'm not sure I fully believe this, but I can't help but wonder if Earthing could help with my high blood pressure.

"So, how did you meet?" Judy asks, looking at Adam and Sheila.

"I met Adam through my husband," Sheila replies. "They were business associates."

"Yeah, so I lost a good friend too," Adam says. "We both miss him a lot."

The rest of the guests then share their stories, and there seems to be one common thread. Everyone was introduced to *ACIM* through a trusted acquaintance at a very difficult time in life.

Everyone but Lilly. She had heard about the course from several renowned authors, and she decided to explore it before anything major went wrong. At least, that's what she thought she was doing.

"And so, by taking the course proactively, I uncovered a tremendous amount of shame, guilt, grief, and fear in my subconscious mind," Lilly concludes. "All because I didn't like and respect myself. You see, I'm gay and open about that, so I assumed I was okay with who I am. However, because of my upbringing, I had internalized a lot of negativity about myself. Until I took the course, I had no idea how much I needed to forgive myself." Forgiveness. There it is again. Really, *ACIM* could have been called a course in forgiveness. True forgiveness, beginning with detachment from the ego's definition of forgiveness. This is the Truth that sets us free.

Judy and I tell our brief stories about *ACIM* and how it is already revealing miracles to us that went unnoticed before. I mention the term *miracle-minded*, and Jordan chuckles.

"Miracle-minded? I love that."

"Well, you should," Judy teases. "He coined it because of you."

"Me?" Jordan says. The others in the circle shift, interested.

"Yeah, you," I say. "I used to think you weren't even aware of it. You would just come in and say something or do something that lit up the room. Now, I think differently. I think you knew exactly what you were doing. You were intentionally lighting up the room by applying *ACIM* in your work."

"I can see that," Adam interjects. "I've worked with Jordan in my business, and I've witnessed the same thing. There is an energy that he channels that is undeniable to anyone who is slightly open-minded and awake. He really is miracle-minded. What an interesting way to put it."

"Well, by now you know the mind is very powerful," Jordan says. "You're right—I'm not winging it when I come into an organization or I'm writing a book. I'm channeling Source Energy. I'm offering myself as an instrument of God's Will. Remember something: We don't work miracles, which is something the ego would want us to think. God works miracles through us. We just have to let Him."

Nicole speaks next. "He uses it in his personal life too. Being miracle-minded isn't something you turn on and off at work. It's a holistic way of life. Everywhere you go, people sense a radiance about you because you see a radiance in them. They may not be able to see the aura, but they feel it. They sense it. The energy is contagious."

Our meeting continues with a reading from the course on forgiveness and atonement. Atonement, or at-One-ment, as it is described, means we're all connected by Source Energy, so anything we do to another human being, we do to ourselves. We are all One. Waking up to this Reality and Truth is what the course is all about.

"I'd like to hear more about how you're applying this at TYPCO, Jack," Tony says. "I'm really struggling with this in my line of work as an attorney."

I nod, while wondering how in the world I can help Tony. If there is one group of people who seem to have a strong attachment to the ego thought-system, it's got to be attorneys. Us-them. Win-lose. Right-wrong. Good-bad. "Well, I'll do what I can to help, Tony. But let me assure you, Jordan is far more experienced at this than I am."

Jordan holds his hand up. "Whoa! Hold on! Can we use this as a learning opportunity?"

We all look at each other.

"Think carefully about what Jack just said," he continues. "What underlying thoughts and assumptions can you uncover from his reply?"

"There's a hint of resistance and doubt," Judy offers after a short silence.

"That's right, Judy," Jordan says. "And where do you think this doubt is coming from?"

"Probably from my subconscious mind," I confess.

Jordan nods. "And why do you have this doubt, Jack?"

"I don't know," I admit. "Probably because I haven't been Earthing enough." Everyone snickers. "No, probably because I think you're better equipped to help Tony than I am. After all, you're the one who helped me."

Jordan asks, "Does anyone else see what's going on here?"

No one says a word. What's he getting at?

"Think about it this way," Nicole hints. "Is Jack's response coming from the ego or the Holy Spirit?"

Aha! It's only the ego that recognizes and experiences feelings of fear and doubt and limitation. The Holy Spirit, available to all of us, is fearless and free. My habitual response reveals my connection to ego, and Jordan immediately picked up on it.

"From the ego," I reply. "Jordan just called me out on a subconscious program I'm running on. I have doubt, projected by the ego, which is nothing more than a self-induced feeling."

"That's right," Jordan says. "There is so much we can learn about one another by the language we use and the words we choose. This is one of the first things you will notice when you make the shift. You will speak differently because you are following a different script."

"So, that's what you do when you come in to help business leaders?" Tony asks, now directing his question to Jordan.

"Yes, that's exactly what I do," he replies. "I approach my work as if I'm simply an extension of the Holy Spirit and an instrument of God's peace. When I do this, failure is not an option."

"Amen to St. Francis!" Lilly adds. "May we all be instruments of God's peace."

Tony takes note. "So, I teach peace by being peace, by embodying it—no matter what anyone else is saying or doing."

I consider this. Yes, this is exactly what I'm beginning to do at TYPCO, and it's already making a difference. The same principle probably applies everywhere. Even a law firm. Jordan's right. I could have answered his question. Somehow, I'm still managing to get in my own way.

PART EIGHT

I Am Spirit

Great spirits have always encountered
violent opposition from mediocre minds.

—**Albert Einstein**

19

The Ego Fights Back

To support mother and father, to cherish partner and children,
and to be engaged in peaceful occupation—
this is the greatest blessing.

—The Buddha

On our drive home from the *ACIM* meeting, I receive a disturbing phone call from my mother. She tells me that my father has just had a heart attack and he is now in recovery at the hospital. My mind races over the past decade, a period when Dad and I have hardly spoken to one another. He has always been a very demanding and forceful man, even late in life, and he never liked it when I disagreed with him. It is his way or the highway. I suppose, in some ways, I adopted the same behavior. We were like two rams butting heads. Eventually, I stopped sharing my experiences with him because I always felt judged and second-guessed. Who needs that?

Fortunately, my mom never gave up on me, and now she tells me that my dad didn't either. "You know he loves you dearly, Jack," she says softly into the phone. "Maybe it's time you two make amends."

"Will that trigger another heart attack?" I ask, somewhat earnestly.

"You have nothing to do with his heart attack," she replies, with a hint of hesitation. "You know he's had high blood pressure and health challenges for years."

"And you don't think that I had anything to do with that?" I probe, carefully watching the road.

"Jack, listen to me," she answers. "What another person says or does cannot affect us unless we allow it to. Your father allowed some people to get under his skin. This is true. And you are no doubt included on that list. So is your brother. But your father could have let it go years ago, and he deliberately chose not to. He found it easier to cast blame and hold grudges. Don't be the same way."

As my mother is saying this, I can't help but think about my own tendencies to follow in my father's footsteps. I guess apples don't fall far from the tree. I'm no different than my father, and yet here I am criticizing him for what I do myself—just like I did with Joe. I think back to the second lesson in *ACIM*: I give meaning to everything I see. I'm giving meaning to my father. And I'm doing essentially nothing to forgive him.

"Okay, Mom. I hear you. Thank you. Do you want me to come to the hospital? I could probably be there in an hour."

"No, there's no need for that tonight. The doctors tell me he's stable. They just want to keep him overnight for observation. I'll stay with him and call you in the morning with an update."

"Okay. Thanks, Mom. I'm here for you if you need anything."

I hang up the phone and glance over at Judy. She's sitting quietly after overhearing our conversation through the Bluetooth.

"What?" I ask.

"I just feel so bad for your mother. She must be terrified."

"Yeah, probably. Although she sounded pretty calm to me. Don't you think?"

She shrugs. "I don't know. Your mom is a strong woman, but this is serious. I can only imagine how I would feel."

We drive in silence for a minute or two, and then Judy asks, "Do you ever talk to your mom about what we're learning in the course?"

"No," I reply abruptly. "I hardly talk to my mom about anything." Another long pause.

"Do you suppose the ego has anything to do with that?"

Ouch! Judy has hit me right between the eyes. When I stop and think about it, the distance I have with my parents is all ego-driven. The same is true with my brother. It's like we're all just trying to protect ourselves. This is the exact opposite of what we were discussing tonight at Jordan's.

"Yes," I admit, shamefully. "In retrospect, this is all about ego preservation. I can see that now. The ego loves a good fight. It keeps it alive."

We drive in silence for another mile or two. I wonder about miracles. My first reaction is to think of Jesus, walking on water and raising people from the dead. Is this what *ACIM* is teaching us to do? Will I be able to use the lessons to heal my father? I must admit, this seems highly doubtful.

"It's interesting what your mom said about letting it go. She said your father could have let go of his hostility years ago, but he chose not to."

"I can relate to that."

"And even so, she loves him unconditionally. She loves him like God loves us, despite what he does."

"That's true love, baby. The kind that's permanent, not temporary. *ACIM* makes that pretty clear."

"Maybe that's where she gets her strength—knowing we're all loved unconditionally, even when we stray from the path."

A distant voice suddenly becomes very clear in my mind. *It's time to walk the talk, Jack. It's time to make amends with your father. What are you waiting for?*

20

I Do Not Understand

All I know is that I know nothing.

—Socrates

The next few days pass, and my father is home with my mother. The doctors have cautioned him to take it easy, but according to my mom, he is just as driven as he always was. My sister came to visit him, and she is now reaching out to me and my brother to make amends. I want to, but there is still something holding me back. Whenever I think about my brother, my blood seems to boil.

"You're in a resistance mode," Jordan says into the phone, after hearing my story. I decided to call him for some insight and advice. "You're resisting flow. It's as simple as that."

"I hear you," I reply, half-heartedly. "But it's awkward. I haven't spoken to my brother or my dad in years."

"That's the ego talking, Jack," Jordan challenges. "By now, you know that. And it's the ego blocking you from Truth. You will never feel at complete peace until you let it go."

I contemplate his words. I suppose my definition of peace is quite different from his. I have moments of peace, usually when I feel victory. But it never seems to last. It's like a glimpse of nirvana, and then I'm back in purgatory, striving for greener grass somewhere else.

"Well, even though I have my differences with my dad, I still love him, and I do want to help. I feel for my mom too. She must be terrified."

"That depends on who she's listening to," he says matter-of-factly. Jordan's answer catches me off guard. "If she's listening to the ego, she will experience fear. If she's listening to the Holy Spirit, she will feel at peace, no matter what." He hesitates for a moment and then adds, "Remember something, Jack. Faith and fear cannot coexist. It's one or the other. True faith means you have complete confidence in the Will of God."

I want to push back, but I don't. I've heard Jordan say this before, and he obviously believes it. If I'm afraid, I've lost faith. Or I've put my faith in fear, which is an illusion. If I have true faith, there is no fear. There is nothing to worry about.

"Come to think of it, my mother didn't really sound terrified when I talked to her on the phone. It's almost like she knows something I don't."

"Maybe she does," Jordan replies. "Ask her and listen to her. Let go of your own agenda and preconceived notions and really listen to her. It sounds like your mom has great faith."

"Yeah, I suppose she does. It's just not a subject we talked about much when I was growing up. We never went to church. And my mom keeps a lot to herself. She's very private." I think back over the years. "She does read a lot of interesting stuff, much of which you might call spiritual."

"Has she shared any of these books with you?"

"No," I reply. "I just remember seeing some of them lying around the house. My father never took the books seriously, and neither did I."

"Well, you don't have to go to a church to be spiritual," Jordan says. "You're already spiritual by nature. We've talked about this. We're all spiritual beings having a temporary human experience. A lot of people see this the other way around, thinking that we're human beings who have temporary spiritual experiences." Again, he pauses to let the words sink in. "So, true spirituality is more about recognizing who we really are and connecting with our higher selves. It's more about remembering and acknowledging who we already are, not attaining some distant goal of enlightenment."

I think again about my mother. She never said much, but her unconditional love and support certainly make me think she is deeply spiritual—and very forgiving.

Jordan continues. "We do this with the help of the Holy Spirit. God is our Source. Some people like to refer to God as Source Energy. Everything comes from this Source Energy. We are the fruit of the vine. We are all in and of God, whole and complete, like rays of the sun. Knowing this brings us great peace and confidence. We live life differently when we believe that we are all One with God. This is what Jesus makes perfectly clear in *ACIM*. God is not separate, which is what the ego would have us think. And we are not separate from one another. We are the Sonship, the body of Christ. And the Holy Spirit is our liaison with God. He is the voice for God, guiding us and teaching us when we ask for help."

"The more you describe this, the more I think of my mother," I interject. "She really is a saint in many ways."

"Talk to her, Jack," Jordan says. "And to your father. Remember, we're all One. Anything you think or say or do to your father, you think or say or do to yourself. Forgiveness sets you free."

"So, do you have any advice on how I might help my father heal?" I ask. "Is there anything *ACIM* can teach me to help my dad mend his heart?"

"Have you been listening? Forgiveness heals the heart. You might want to start with that."

"Are you saying my forgiveness heals my dad's heart?"

"No," he says firmly. "Your forgiveness heals your heart. There is nothing you can do to heal your father, other than influence his belief system. It is his belief system that determines his outcomes."

"What about the doctors?" I continue. "Can't they heal him?"

"Doctors can treat him," Jordan explains. "They cannot heal him. Only his beliefs can heal him."

I think about my own heart condition and high blood pressure. Despite being treated by doctors and prescribed medications, none of these things are healing me. They might be keeping my body alive, but my blood pressure is still high. And they are doing nothing to heal my mind.

"Of course, when a doctor treats a patient, it can influence his beliefs," he adds. "This is often referred to as the placebo effect. If we think we're healing, it helps accelerate the process. On the other hand, if we believe a doctor when he tells us we have three months to live, we accelerate our passing. Dr. Bruce Lipton refers to this as the 'nocebo effect.'"

"Ha," I say. "I've never heard of that before. The nocebo effect?"

"Yes, it's simply a negative spin on the placebo effect," he says. "Put simply, be careful what you believe, no matter where it's coming from. Miracles do not come from negativity and resistance. On the contrary, they come from open-minded flow and faith."

"So, I really can't do anything to help my dad except influence his beliefs?"

"That's correct," he replies. "But you can do that. It all starts with forgiveness. Listen to your heart. Forgiveness will set you free. It is a form of letting go. It releases toxic thoughts and energy from the mind and body—consciously and unconsciously—which is very healthy. You can influence your father by demonstrating courage, compassion, and inner peace—all through forgiveness. Be the change, Jack. Be the example. It is the only thing you have any real control over."

PART NINE

By Grace I Live

If you want others to be happy, practice compassion.
If you want to be happy, practice compassion.
—His Holiness the Dalai Lama

21

Synchronicity

Don't dismiss the synchronicity of what is happening right
now finding its way to your life at just this moment.
There are no coincidences in the universe,
only convergences of Will, Intent and Experience.

—Neale Donald Walsch

Back at home with Judy, I summarize my conversation with Jordan. I admit that I'm still very much attached to the ego thought-system, and this is influencing how I feel about my dad, my brother, my work, myself, and my whole life.

"Just when I think I'm beginning to understand these lessons from the course, I get thrown a curveball," I confess. "Apparently, the programming runs pretty deep."

"Well, we're only about a month into it," she says softly. "We probably have to give it more time."

"I know, but you know me. I want results quickly."

"Sounds like the ego talking again."

No sooner does she say this than I realize it myself. In fact, I bet I would have recognized this voice even if she didn't say anything. Maybe this is what awakening and becoming more conscious is all about. Maybe it's about recognizing the ego when it speaks and then dismissing it.

I chuckle. "You're right. I knew it the moment I said it."

She smiles. "You're becoming more present and aware, honey. That's a solid first step. At least, that's what Nicole told me. I talked with her again today on the phone."

"Really?" I say. "That's nice. What else did she have to say?"

"Well, she said that we would soon need to shift from the 'what' to the 'how.' She said this is a struggle for many people. They know what to do. They just don't know how."

"Makes sense." I sigh. "I see that all the time at work."

"So, we have to learn how to let go of the ego thought-system. Now that we know what it is and how misleading it can be, we have to detach from it."

"Like breaking a habit?"

"Yes, that's exactly how Nicole explained it. As humans, we're creatures of habit. Remember, most of our lives are run on auto-pilot, by the subconscious mind. We just keep replaying the same old tapes repeatedly."

"Sounds like Einstein's definition of insanity. Doing the same thing over and over and expecting different results."

"Very true. And by now you know how often the course refers to the ego as completely insane. The idea that we're separate from God and from one another is crazy."

"Yeah. This is one of the most troubling lessons in the course for me. So much of what we consider sane in our society—socially, economically, financially, professionally, politically, physically, emotionally, judicially—is completely insane when viewed through the Holy Spirit. The ego has us blindfolded and brainwashed."

"Yes, it does. And if we try to make sense of the course through the eyes and ears of the ego, we will never get it."

"That's brilliant on the ego's part."

The sound of Judy's laughter reminds me of our first date when we went to a comedy show. She sounds gentle and innocent. Like she's experiencing pure joy. Her ability to get to that point is one of the things I love most about her. "That's why we have to detach from it and let it go rather than fight it," she explains. "Nicole made this very clear. It's our only way out of a thought-system that has preserved itself since the fall from grace."

"When humankind saw itself as separate from God."

"And from one another," she adds. "When we see one another as separate, rather than beings of light sourced by God, we deny our holiness. We then live in a perpetual state of guilt."

"Reminds me of how *ACIM* describes arrogance. Arrogance is not proclaiming our Oneness with God. It's denying it. It's the ego that is arrogant."

Judy nods. "So, now we have to learn how to let go of our attachment to the ego thought-system. We both know what we need to do. The next question is how."

"Yes, how," I mumble. "Isn't the course supposed to teach us that?"

"It will," Judy replies. "At least, that's what Nicole said. We just need to be patient and continue to practice the lessons every day. I'm just wondering if there are other tools we can use to help. You know, like habit-breaking tools."

With that, Judy picks up the television remote and clicks on the TV. "Do you mind if I watch one of my shows?"

"What? No music?" I kid.

She giggles. "Maybe later, if you play your cards right."

"Watch whatever you want, baby," I say, getting up from the couch and heading to the kitchen. "I have plenty of work to do."

Minutes later, Judy is tuned into Dr. Oz, and she is beckoning me to join her. "Come here, Jack. You have to see this."

I return to the couch and begin watching. One of Dr. Oz's guests is a *New York Times* bestselling author by the name of Nick Ortner. He is demonstrating a release technique called EFT—Emotional Freedom Technique. It combines the ancient Chinese healing practice of acupressure with modern-day psychology. He also refers to EFT as Tapping.

"This is interesting," I say. "And timely. We were just talking about learning how to let go of habits and limiting beliefs."

"This is no coincidence, Jack," she whispers, shushing me. "This is a sign."

We watch in silence for the next ten minutes while EFT is being demonstrated. Apparently, there are nine electrical meridians in our bodies that we tap on while reciting a release phrase. These meridians are like circuit breakers in an electrical box. If the circuits are tripped, we're going to have problems. We can change the light bulbs all day, but they will not light until we reset the circuit.

Ortner explains that the body is very electrical. The brain is electrical. The nervous system is electrical. The heart is electromagnetic. However, most medical treatments in the Western world are chemical. We have drugs for everything but very few electrical treatments. EFT offers us an option. By tapping on the nine meridians, one at a time, and reciting carefully scripted phrases, we are releasing blockages. These blockages could be the result of trauma, disease, negative experiences, upbringing, or any limiting beliefs.

"I wonder if this will work on releasing the ego," I whisper.

"We can try it," Judy replies. "First, let's learn how to do it."

Ortner identifies the nine meridians on the body: There is the side of the hand, or karate-chop point. Either hand is fine.

He then moves to the inside of the eyebrow, closest to the bridge of the nose. From here, he taps on the outside of the eye bone near the temple, followed by the bone just under the eye. Again, either eye is acceptable. He then taps on the bone just beneath the nose and above the mouth. The next stop is right under the mouth, above the chin. From here, he goes to the collarbone, either side, and then to a spot about four inches below the armpit. He finishes by tapping on the top of his head.

While he is tapping, he recites the phrase "Even though I have this [fear] or [tendency to do something], I totally and completely love and forgive and accept myself." We can fill in the bracketed places with whatever we want to release. It can be a fear, a pain, a bad habit, an emotion, anything weighing us down.

"I wonder if this will work on letting go of the ego," I repeat.

"I think it is worth a try. Why not?"

"So, our set-up phrase could be something like 'Even though I'm attached to the ego, I totally and completely accept myself.'"

"Sure," she says. "Or, 'Even though I have a tendency to get stressed, I completely love and forgive myself.'"

"Ortner said we can phrase it in different ways. We just have to be brutally honest with ourselves."

"We can even use humor," Judy adds. "So, you could say, 'Even though I've been a complete jerk to my dad and my brother, I totally love and appreciate myself.'"

"Ouch," I tease, knowing she is playing with me.

"This is fascinating. And not just the technique but the fact that it showed up today on our television."

I consider the timing and spiritual connection. "Jordan refers to this as synchronicity. He said it's one of the first signs of enlightenment. These cosmic coincidences are happening all the time, but most of us are too dense or preoccupied to notice."

22

The Truth Sets Me Free

A mind unruffled by vagaries of fortune, from sorrow freed,
from defilements cleansed, from fear liberated—
this is the greatest blessing.

—**The Buddha**

As I sit alone in our conference room at TYPCO, preparing for another staff meeting, I practice another meditation technique. I got here early just to do this. Why not add meditation to my preparation protocol? I may even offer it to my executive team as part of our culture change.

Today's method is another one Judy taught me. She learned it from Nicole. It's a Taoist practice I can do anywhere. To facilitate flow, or the great current, as the Taoists call it, I simply close my eyes, deepen my breathing, and direct my attention to various parts of my body. I then tell each part to relax. So, for example, I can start by focusing my attention on my heart and saying, "Heart of mine, relax." I can then move to my eyes, my ears, my elbows, my knees, my back, my brain, or any place that ails me. As I breathe through my organs and limbs and bones and skin, focusing on relaxation, I am boosting my circulation and immune system. I'm also quieting the mind and teaching it to relax. I like this method because it's simple and effective and I can do it anywhere. I can even do it while I swim laps, which is another change I am making in my life. I stop at the health club three days a week now on my way to work.

Our meeting this morning has an item on the agenda that I am especially interested in. Joe is to report on his progress preparing for our upcoming kaizen event on customer service. As usual, my executive team shuffles into the room without any real sense of urgency or purpose. I watch each member as they take a seat, and I find myself once again in critical mode. Why do I do this? Why am I so judgmental? I tell myself to relax. I also remind myself to look for the light of God in my team members. Rather than focus on what I don't like, I choose to find things I do like. When I see the Christ in others, they begin to see the Christ in me.

Joe updates everyone on the progress he's making with the kaizen team. The team has been selected, trained by Jordan, and is now in data-collection mode. The kaizen event week is still two weeks out, and it triggers a lot of questions from my staff.

"So, Joe, why are we expected to be at these briefings each day?" Scott asks, looking from Joe to me.

"Think of this like the television show *Undercover Boss*," Joe replies. "If you haven't seen the show, it's about different CEOs who go undercover to experience their own businesses." A few heads nod with recognition. "These CEOs often experience some pretty painful moments, most of which have been hidden from them by members of their staff. In other words, they learn things about their own businesses they never knew before."

"Are you saying we hide things from Jack?" a member of my team asks.

Joe is quick to respond. "No, that's not what I am saying at all. I'm saying that there are probably things going on in this business that we should know about as an executive team, but we don't. For whatever reason, we are missing valuable information."

"Like what?" another member asks defensively. "We have more metrics than any company I know."

Joe grins and looks at me. "Like why we get so many customer phone calls and complaints," he says. "And why our NPS is so low."

Immediately, the defensiveness and finger-pointing begin. Joe isn't five minutes into his presentation, and all hell breaks loose. I suddenly remember a technique Jordan used during his briefings. He has a couple of key ground rules that are very helpful.

I speak up confidently but without jumping into the fire. "May I suggest a couple of ground rules while Joe is presenting?"

The clamor dies down, and all heads now turn toward me. "Let's try this. Rule number one: Joe gets ten minutes to present without any interruptions. You can hold your questions and comments until he is through with his presentation. Joe, that means ten minutes, not twenty or thirty. Keep it brief and to the point." Joe nods in agreement. "Rule number two: When we do open it up for discussion, you cannot challenge Joe unless you have facts and data to back up your argument. We are not going to debate with opinions. Joe, that means you need to present with facts and data as well."

The room goes silent. This changes a lot. Normally, we interrupt one another, arguing over assumptions and beliefs without any factual data. I can feel the tension and anxiety around the table wane. Georgia looks at me and smiles.

For the next ten minutes, Joe gets right to the point, and he appears to answer all the questions that would have interrupted him without the new rule. As a result, there are very few questions or comments at the end.

"Makes sense to me," Scott says, looking at Joe. "Nicely done."

"I like it," Georgia adds. "I think this analysis will be quite telling. Plus, I love the idea of having our own associates do the work rather than a bunch of consultants. What a wonderful opportunity for them!"

The meeting continues for another thirty minutes, and we finish early for the first time in my tenure as president. What a change! The room empties, and I continue to sit for a moment. Georgia is halfway out the door when she does an about-face and walks over to me.

"Do you have a few minutes, Jack?" she asks.

"Sure," I reply, pointing to the chair next to me. "Sit down."

Georgia takes a seat and looks at me with concern. "Are you okay?"

I smile. "Yeah, I'm good. What makes you ask?"

She shakes her head and looks at the ceiling. "I don't know. It just seems like there is something going on. And I'm not the only one who thinks so. People are talking. We're wondering if you're okay."

"I see."

"I mean, we know your father is ill, and that probably weighs on you," she explains. "But you seem like a different person."

"In what kind of way?"

She hesitates, appearing to choose her words carefully. "You aren't as demanding and controlling and intense as you usually are. You seem more centered and relaxed."

"Is that bad?"

"No, not at all," she answers with a laugh. "It's refreshing. You're setting a different tone for everyone. I like it. I just want to make sure you aren't giving up on us."

"Well, thank you, Georgia. Let's just say I'm learning to see things differently. And I'm definitely not giving up on anyone, especially you."

She gets up to leave. "Well, whatever it is you're learning, I want to learn it too. It appears to be a blessing."

PART TEN

Love Is the Way

The heart has reasons that reason cannot know.

—Blaise Pascal

23

Lead Us Not into Temptation

The world is afflicted by death and decay. But the wise do not
grieve, having realized the nature of the world.

—**The Buddha**

My mother speaks softly into the phone. "Jack, you know your
father loves you."

"Yes, I do, Mom," I reply, reflecting on some of the lessons in
ACIM. Despite my father's gruff character and insistence on control, I envision the light of God shining through him. We are all one
with God, innocent because of our ignorance.

"And he's only wanted the very best for you and your brother
and sister," she adds. "Maybe he didn't always show this, but trust
me, he would have done anything for you."

I think back over the years, reflecting on the countless argu-
ments and debates we had. Why did he have to be so hard on me?
What was driving him? It was like I was his prize racehorse being
trained and conditioned to compete and win. I felt more like a tro-
phy than a son.

"How is he feeling now?" I ask.

"He's resting and feeling a bit better," she replies. "He's very glad to be home from the hospital. You know he doesn't like hospitals."

I know he doesn't like a lot of things. Spend ten minutes with my dad, and you will hear a continuous stream of grievances. The phone company is messed up. The government is scandalous. The school system is a problem. Homeless people are a problem. Healthcare is a scam. Blah, blah, blah.

"Yeah, I know. It seems he doesn't like a lot of things."

"Well, you never have to guess what your father is thinking." She laughs. "He tells it like he sees it."

I think about this. He tells it like he sees it. So, he must see a lot of negative in the world. *ACIM* refers to this as grievances and attack thoughts. And grief carries a very low, unhealthy frequency, according to David Hawkins. It weighs very heavy on the heart.

"I guess you're right, Mom. You never have to guess how Dad is feeling."

"It's just too bad he thinks he has no control over his feelings," she continues. "There's no doubt in my mind that his pessimism contributes to his heart disease."

Whoa, I didn't expect to hear this from my mother. "Do you really believe that?"

"I do," she says without hesitation. "I believe we reap what we sow. We get out of life what we put into it. So, on the one hand, if we're feeling uneasy, anxious, or afraid, it's because we're looking at things negatively. This can easily translate into anger and even depression—which is simply anger turned inward. On the other hand, if we focus on the positive, we will feel excited, inspired, and eager for more. We will feel more appreciation and gratitude in life, which is very healthy."

I remember Nicole saying that appreciation and gratitude are two very high-frequency energies, and they are one of the quickest ways to transcend the negative, ego way of thinking.

My mother continues. "If there's one thing I've learned over the years, Jack, it's that our bodies respond to what our minds are thinking. There are even some amazing scientific experiments to prove this now. We discuss them in my book club. In fact, our thoughts influence our DNA, and our DNA influences the field of energy around us. This explains why some people seem to light up the room. They channel a very enlightening energy."

I sit in silence, somewhat stunned. I had no idea my mother knew anything about this. My father ran the show when we were growing up, and my mother was reluctant to disagree with him— at least hesitant to do so out loud, and definitely not in front of anyone. She dropped out of college to be a dancer, but she then gave up her dreams to get married and raise a family. So, she must have learned a lot of this through self-study. I decide to investigate. Maybe it's time I learn a little more about my mother.

"Where did you learn this, Mom?"

I can feel her gentle smile over the phone. "I read a lot. You know that. And I practice what I learn. I experiment. Information doesn't do us any good if we don't apply it—and turn it into knowledge and understanding."

I nod as if she can see me. "So, why do you suppose Dad is so resistant to this? I'm sure you must discuss it."

"Yes, well, when the student is ready, the teacher will appear," she replies. "Your father isn't ready."

"And you're okay with this? Aren't you feeling a bit anxious and afraid?"

She hesitates before answering. "No, I'm not afraid. I have great faith, Jack. Even though we never really talk about it. I love your father, and we've had a wonderful life together. I believe happiness is a choice, not a chance occurrence. That's why I've always chosen happiness, even in my dark hours. I choose to see positive where a lot of people see negative. When there's a natural disaster, for example, I see all the people coming to help. When I see people make mistakes, I see lessons being learned. The world is full of negative and positive, what some refer to as a perfect yin-yang balance. Everything in the universe is in perfect harmony. So, we must ask ourselves, do we see the glass half-empty or half-full? Your father and I disagree on a lot of things, but we still love each other, no matter what."

"Mom, I have to say I'm somewhat surprised by how casually you seem to be taking this. Dad is not well. It seems most people in your situation would be terrified."

She hesitates for a moment and then offers this: "That's because most people don't think the way I do. It all boils down to our beliefs and our faith."

"Can I ask what you believe about this?"

"Of course," she replies, her tone soft and sweet. "I have nothing to hide. I believe your father came to this planet for a reason, and he will soon return to where he came from, his true home."

Hearing Mom reference Dad's death as an imminent event gives me a strange feeling. Despite myself, I feel queasy, and I have to work hard to focus on her words as she continues.

"This is the real circle of life. We are eternal beings. There is no death. Our experience on earth is really just a chance for our souls to develop and express themselves." She takes a deep breath. "So, why should I be afraid? If anything, I feel comforted knowing that your father will be returning home to heaven. His life here has been like a living hell."

Again, I'm stunned by my mother's commentary. "Why do you say that?"

"Because all he tends to see is negative. And it affects him physically, emotionally, mentally, and socially. I've witnessed this for years, Jack, and it's painful to see."

I feel a surge of compassion come over me. "I will come see him, Mom. Definitely within the next week."

"Good," she whispers. "Whether he admits it or not, I think he'll appreciate it."

By forgiving my father, I'm forgiving myself. I'm setting myself free.

24

Deliver Us from Ego

> Appreciation is a wonderful thing;
> it makes what is excellent in others belong to us as well.
>
> —**Voltaire**

The trip down to Cape Cod is relatively smooth. It's off-season, so most summer residents and tourists have moved on. My parents moved to the Cape a few years ago when my dad retired. They now live a simple life in a small house in a quaint town called Osterville.

My mother informed my dad that we were coming for a visit, and he didn't object. Hopefully, our reunion goes more smoothly than I expect. Maybe I've been reading him all wrong. Maybe he does want to reconcile.

Judy seems to read my mind as we turn onto my parent's street. "You have doubts about this visit, don't you?"

"Yeah, I guess I do," I admit. "It's just so awkward. My dad and I haven't spoken in years."

"Well, for whatever it's worth, remember what we're learning in the course. If you're feeling anxious and afraid, it's because you're projecting negativity from the ego. You're creating a self-fulfilling prophecy."

"I know. It's just another one of those habitual tendencies I have to change."

"And you will. Think about some of the good times you've had with your father. Surely you can think of some. And look for the light of Christ in him. It's there, and he loves you. You just need to look for it. Forget about all the crap you've been carrying around in your mind and let go of your resistance and defensiveness. What is it you like to say? Let go and let flow?"

I glance at Judy. "You're right. I'm probably my own worst enemy in this situation."

"We all get in our own way from time to time. Let's use this moment to witness a miracle with your dad. What does the course call that? The Holy Instant?"

"Yes, the Holy Instant. It's when we experience a shift in perception, from ego-thinking to forgiveness. We see the light of Christ in one another and our Oneness with God."

"Okay. So, lets visualize this reunion going extremely well. Imagine you and your dad hugging and apologizing and truly forgiving your mishaps and stubbornness as if they never happened."

"I suppose I can do that."

"Good," Judy says with enthusiasm. "I'm excited about this. I feel really good."

We pull into my parents' driveway, and the two of them are standing there waiting for us. My father has his arm around my mom and a stern look on his face. My mother is grinning from ear to ear.

I get out of the car and walk up to them, first giving my mother a big hug. I then turn to my dad and offer him a hug as well. He looks at me hesitantly and then seems to surrender to my offer.

We embrace for what seems like minutes, and I almost begin to cry. Can forgiveness be this easy? We haven't even said a word.

My mother watches us with tears in her eyes, and Judy starts tearing up as well. A Holy Instant. Pure letting go.

"I've missed you, Dad," I whisper, my arms releasing their grip.

"I've missed you too, son," he replies. "More than you know."

"That was quite a scare," I say, looking into his dark-brown eyes. "Did you have any idea it was coming?"

"Not at all. Seems like it just came out of nowhere. I guess the old ticker finally hit a tock."

I grin. "Well, I'm glad you're still here. I think we have a lot to catch up on."

We walk into the house and sit down in the living room. My mom and Judy join us minutes later with a tray of tea and coffee and pastries. When Judy sets the tray on the coffee table, I notice a book lying there. It's called *Proof of Heaven*, by neurosurgeon Eben Alexander.

"Is this one of the books you're reading, Mom?" I ask, picking up the book.

"Yes, it is," she replies enthusiastically. "It's a *New York Times* bestseller. Fascinating story about life after death. I'm reading it to your father."

My dad acknowledges my mom's comment with a nod.

"You like it, Dad?" I ask, trying to open a positive conversation.

He hesitates as if to think about it. Here we go again. He will probably find something wrong with it. Suddenly, I catch myself. Why do I think that? Why do I assume the negative? I'm no different than my father when I do that. And that's the very thing I tend to criticize.

He surprises me with his answer. "Actually, I really do like it. It's an amazing story."

"We'll have to add that to our reading list, Jack," Judy suggests. "I'm always up for a good read."

"Oh, you'll love this book," my mom says. "You can have our copy when we're done with it."

Judy and I look at each other as if to ask, is this a miracle? Judy then turns to my mother and says, "That's so nice, Rosemary. I'd like to hear more about your book club and some of the other books you're reading. Jack tells me you have quite a list."

For the next two hours, we catch up on all kinds of things. My mom tells us about some of her favorite books, and my father fills me in on his retirement activities. I also share my life story about work and family, and Judy does the same. It turns out my father had no idea I was promoted to president of a major TYPCO business unit.

"Well, congratulations, Jack," he says when hearing the news. "That's quite an accomplishment."

"Thanks, Dad. I took quite a few risks in my old position as GM, and it seems our progress didn't go unnoticed. Now, I'm being tasked to boost the performance and change the culture of an entire business unit."

"When you say culture, what exactly do you mean by that?" He appears genuinely interested.

"It's essentially the way we do things around there. It's like a corporate personality resulting in specific behaviors. You might even call it a field of energy or a vibration. Some company cultures are slow and dysfunctional and confusing—like my business unit is now. Others are lean, harmonized, creative, and flowing, which is what we're aiming for. My task is to lead the charge. It's like changing habits at an organizational level. Not an easy task or quick fix."

"And that's what you did in your prior job?"

"Yes, sir. It is." I pause. "Well, actually, I didn't do it alone. We did it together as a team. I simply helped steer the process."

"That's fascinating, Jack," my mother says. "We all know how hard it can be for people to change habits. Imagine doing it for a whole company."

"I suppose that's what true leadership is all about," my father says. "It reminds me of some great coaches who turn their sports teams around, from losers to winners. They develop a whole new mind-set."

"That's right, Dad. Good analogy. They make believers out of people."

"I've always been fascinated by that," he admits. "It's quite a gift. And now my son is doing it. I'm proud of you, Jack."

I glance over at Judy, who is now beaming. So is my mother. And when I look back at my father, I see not only a smile on his weathered face but a hint of light around his head. For the first time in my life, I see my father's aura.

PART ELEVEN

My Holy Instant

Our greatest glory is not in never falling,
but in rising up every time we fall.
—Oliver Goldsmith

25

The Wisdom of Emptiness

First of all, there will appear to you, swifter than lightning,
the luminous splendor of the colorless light of emptiness,
and that will surround you on all sides . . . Try to submerge
yourself in that light, giving up all belief in a separate self,
all attachment to your illusory ego.

—Buddhist teaching

During the next week, my father and I talk several times by
phone. He seems to be intensely curious about my work, and he
appears to be even more intrigued with the way I am handling it.
I think back to when I first met Jordan and how intrigued I was with
his approach. Maybe my dad is wondering the same thing about
me now. Rather than pushing, I am pulling. Rather than dictating
with my old command-and-control authority, which I learned from
him, I am using positive influence and intrigue to inspire change
through teams. I have even invited my dad to TYPCO to see what
we're doing.

Since reuniting with him, I also feel as if a great weight has been
lifted from my shoulders. And my heart. I feel more inner peace.
I feel more grace. I feel more confidence. The distance between us

was clearly unhealthy, and I thank God for our reconciliation. Especially now.

It's 6:05 AM, and my mother is calling. Something is wrong.

"Good morning, Mom," I say softly into the phone. "What's up?"

She's crying. "I'm sorry to call so early, but I have some news."

I set my latest attempt at a morning smoothie down on the kitchen table next to my gym bag and sit down.

She continues, sniffling between breaths. "Your father has passed. He must have passed during the night. I didn't know until just now. He's not breathing. Jack, he's gone."

I sit quietly for a moment, feeling numb. How can this be? The doctors said he was in the clear. We had just reconciled. We were making plans together. Suddenly, I can feel anger rising within me, but I don't seem to care. How is this fair? How is this just? I want to scream at someone.

Instinctively, I spring into action, taking charge and telling my mom what to do. "I'm on my way, Mom. Sit tight. We'll get through this together."

"Thank you," she whispers. "I thought I was prepared for this, but it's so sudden."

Yes, it is. And somebody should pay for it.

. . . .

By the time Judy and I arrive at my mother's house, she has had my father's body taken to the morgue, and she is sitting quietly in her garden, sipping a cup of tea and listening to the songbirds. She looks almost angelic. I sit down next to her and hold her hand. Judy does the same on the other side.

"How are you feeling, Mom?" I ask.

She lets out a long sigh. "Well, I miss him already. We've been together for a very long time."

I try to imagine how this must feel. "Well, you're not alone. You know that, right? We're here for you."

"Yes, we are, Rosemary," Judy adds, squeezing her hand gently.

"Oh, I know that," she says. "Thank you. Your presence means a lot to me."

We sit quietly for a moment, and then I feel compelled to challenge the situation, as if I can change it. Judy warned me about maintaining my cool on our drive down from Boston, but I can't seem to help myself. I'm angry and frustrated. Even though I vented quite a bit in the car, I have to say something.

"So, I thought Dad was in the clear, Mom."

She nods, tears welling up in her eyes. "I did too."

I expect her to say more, but she doesn't. She just sits there, gracefully. Maybe I expect her to get angry with me. I glance at Judy, who gives me that look that says, *Calm down. Breathe deeply, Jack. Meditate. Relax. Remember what we're learning in* ACIM.

I ignore it. "So, what exactly did the doctors say when Dad left the hospital?"

Mom sits for a moment, as if contemplating my question, and then she replies, "What does it matter?"

"What does it matter? It matters a lot. What if the doctors screwed up? What if we were given misleading information? What if . . . ?"

"Maybe your father decided it was time to go," she says, wiping away a tear. "Who knows?"

What? I almost bite my tongue. "Aren't you angry? Maybe Dad could still be alive."

Judy is now staring at me, her eyes sending a very clear message. Apparently, I've lost control, reverting to my old egotistical self.

Again, my mother surprises me. "He is alive, Jack. He has simply returned to heaven."

I want to argue, but somehow, I seem to be making things worse by trying to help. How ironic is that? My mother is going to be so lonely. After all these years of living with him, her husband is gone. Who is going to take care of her now? Who is going to make her laugh—and probably cry? And fix her tea? And a million other things?

She says, "I know I'm going to miss his physical presence, but the way I see it, I'm never alone. Even when I'm by myself, I feel the Holy Spirit's presence. I've felt it for years. And I will feel your father's presence too."

I think of *ACIM*. "Mom, can I ask you something?"

"Sure," she replies. "You know you can."

"Well, you read a lot," I continue. "Have you ever come across something called *A Course in Miracles*?"

She laughs softly, wiping away another tear. Judy hands her a fresh tissue. "Funny you should ask. You're probably the fifth person to ask me that question in the past week. No, I haven't taken the course, but I am familiar with it. Why do you ask?"

Now I laugh, the anger slowly subsiding. "Judy and I are taking it. A lot of what you're saying is in the course."

"Well, that's reassuring. Maybe I'm not so crazy after all."

"No, you're not. And I appreciate what you have to say about faith and the Holy Spirit and all that. How come we never talked about this when I was growing up?"

"Probably . . . because you and your father didn't want to hear it. And probably because I didn't know much about it at the time. I still don't. I guess we just keep getting tested every day. That's how we learn."

She's right. We are getting tested, and clearly, I am struggling with today's lesson. My dad's passing really has set me back. It's like everything I've learned in the course has gone right out the window. The ego has taken over, and I am swimming in grief, anger, and attack.

My mom squeezes my hand. "For whatever it's worth, Jack, I knew the last time I saw you that something was different. You may not yet see it yourself, or appreciate it, but I know you. You're changing. You're learning to lighten up."

Interesting, I think to myself. What a testimonial.

"Your father noticed it too," she adds. "He couldn't stop talking about it."

Hmmm. That's an even greater testimonial. "What did he say?"

"Oh, things like how proud he is of you and how accomplished you are. But most of all, he talked about how at peace you seem to be. You don't get defensive and worked up like you used to, even when he pushes your buttons."

I laugh, thinking of my dad. "He certainly knew how to push my buttons."

"Yes, he did." She chuckles. "Mine, too. Where do you think my motivation came from to learn a lot of this stuff? Without your father testing me all the time, I never would have persisted in finding inner peace."

Now that's quite an impressive way to look at the situation. Rather than getting defensive and upset, my mom learned to control her response to my father when he agitated her. She didn't fight with him. She danced with him, knowing that beneath his egocentric ways, there was a soul yearning to be loved—and saved. That's pure wisdom and grace, if you ask me. And I never saw it in my mother until now.

"Did I ever tell you I went to see the Dalai Lama speak?" she asks.

"No, Mom, you never told me that."

"Yes, it was several years ago, and he was lecturing at Indiana University, where his brother used to teach. Some friends of mine from my book club invited me to go with them, so I jumped on the opportunity. As it turned out, it was very timely. The Dalai Lama was speaking on the wisdom of emptiness and detachment, something I really needed to hear at the time. He said that many people go through life with their cups overflowing. This results in feelings of being overwhelmed, anxious, and stressed. It also means that you cannot receive anything more in your cup because it's already full."

"I can relate to that." I sigh, thinking of my massive to-do list.

"So can I," Judy whispers.

My mother continues. "I think in some ways we all can. That's the ego's modus operandi. More, more, more. Anyway, I walked away from that lecture with some great takeaways. Evidently, there was a lot I needed to let go of, including my attachment to your father."

"What do you mean by that?" I ask.

Again, she laughs as if at herself. "Well, I used to think that I could only be happy if your father was happy. I was attaching my happiness to something I couldn't control."

"And Dad wasn't making that easy for you, right?"

"Not at all. But rather than get angry and defensive and try to change your father, I decided to view it as him teaching me to change myself. He was who he was. We all are. The only thing we can really do is be the best person we can be, regardless of how others act."

"So, you see Dad as a teacher?"

"We're all teachers, Jack," Mom says without hesitation. "We teach what we demonstrate. It reminds me of that take on something Ralph Waldo Emerson said, 'What you do speaks so loudly

I cannot hear what you are saying.' And by teaching, we're learning. We're reinforcing what we believe. The Dalai Lama said that some of our greatest teachers are the people who test us the most, including ourselves."

"So, what did you do?" I ask. "How did you detach?"

"Oh, I learned some meditation and release techniques, and I just kept practicing. And praying."

"Mom, this is so close to home for us right now I can't believe we're talking about it. Thank you for sharing this. I think we have a lot more to share."

"Yes, thank you, Rosemary," Judy says.

"My pleasure. Maybe this is your father's way of bringing us all closer together. Oh, and by the way, if it's okay with you, I'd like you to give his eulogy. I know you will speak from your heart."

I squeeze her hand gently. "Of course, Mom. Whatever you want."

While I maintain a kind expression, my thoughts swirl. I might need some help with this.

PART TWELVE

Let Me Remember

It is under the greatest adversity that there exists the greatest
potential for doing good, both for oneself and others.

—His Holiness the Dalai Lama

26

Transcendence, Atonement, and Salvation

> Those who cling to perceptions and views
> wander the world offending people.
>
> —**The Buddha**

As I sit quietly in my mother's study, drafting a eulogy for my father, I can't help but think about some of the things she said. The wisdom of emptiness. The sanctity of letting go. Loving without attachment. Transcendence. Atonement. Salvation. Some of this might be good for the eulogy. I scribble a few notes.

ACIM teaches us to be present and mindful of the eternal now. It is the only time that really matters. In fact, it is the only time that ever actually exists. The past is past, and the future isn't here yet. We live in the now. And our emotions, whatever they might be, tell us if we are in flow or not. When we feel good, we are aligned with Source Energy and we are present. When we feel bad, we are resisting Source Energy and we are not present. So, *we* don't work miracles. Miracles work through us when we surrender to God—and to the moment. We are simply the vehicles or facilitators. Jesus was able to channel the healing power of Source Energy through to other people by being present, awake, and aware. He was far beyond the limits of the ego thought-system.

The law of attraction teaches us that we don't have to chase our dreams. If we simply maintain a happy, positive vibration, our dreams will find us. All we need to do is decide what we want, focus on it, pay attention to the field, and act on the opportunities when they present themselves. These synchronicities are happening all the time.

My brother, David, and my sister, Caroline, are due in town any minute, so I quickly scribble down a few more thoughts. It would be nice to include them in whatever I say. I just don't want to offend anyone, especially at a funeral.

David and I have the same kind of love-hate relationship we had with my dad. Plus, we all got busy with our careers and families, so we fell out of touch. Now, when I think about it, I kick myself. I haven't been the best big brother in the world. And the more I reflect, the more I realize that ego had everything to do with the breakdown in our relationship. It was always about who is right and who is wrong. Attack and defend. Criticize and judge. Condemn and walk away. There were just so many things about my brother I didn't approve of. He was the happy-go-lucky one, and I was the serious, hard worker. He was the son who ran off and squandered what he had, and I was the son who stayed home and took care of things.

Suddenly, it hits me. I'm jealous and resentful of David. These are two more ego traits. When I compare myself to my brother, I envy him in some ways. I remember getting really upset when he acted irresponsibly, but I admired his sense of adventure, curiosity, and fearlessness. He just never knew it. Perhaps, deep down, I was worried about him. He would tell me to lighten up, and I thought he was being careless. Maybe he was trying to be helpful. I recall wanting to say the same thing to my dad. *Lighten up, Dad. I can take care of this.* I didn't mean to offend him. I meant to help him.

Caroline often got caught in the middle, and as much as she tried, she struggled as a mediator. That was probably my fault too. I didn't make it easy for her. Besides, she generally sided with David, so I felt like it was two against one. It will be interesting to see how they act now, with Dad's passing.

I scribble down a few more thoughts and then hear voices coming from the kitchen. It sounds like my siblings have arrived. I am about to get up and head to the kitchen when the door swings open and my mother walks in, followed by David and Caroline.

Without saying a word, I stand and look at my brother and sister. For an instant, I feel like crying. A rush of emotion comes over me and I walk over to give them each a hug, beginning with my sister. When I step back and look at them again, they have tears in their eyes. Is this because of Dad's passing, or is it something else? Do I have something to do with the tears?

I glance at my mother. Her eyes are glistening as well. When I look back at my brother, he is gesturing for another hug. We embrace silently for a second time. So much for words. Maybe hugging is an easier way to express forgiveness. Finally, I whisper, "I've missed you, David."

"I've missed you too, Jack," he says softly. "It's been way too long."

"Can I get another hug?" Caroline says, putting her arms out to me. "I've missed you too!"

I give my sister a giant bear hug, almost lifting her off her feet.

"Well, maybe this is a blessing from your father," my mother says, holding my brother's hand. "After all, it was his last wish."

"He actually said that, Mom?" I ask.

"Yes, he did." She sniffs. "He was very clear about that. He wanted his family back together. We talked about it the night before he passed."

"I'm so sorry, Mom," my sister says, reaching for her other hand. "I feel terrible."

"Oh, don't fret, Caroline. That's the last thing your father wanted. We had many discussions about life and death, and he said whoever goes first is going to get one heck of a party."

My brother lights up. "I guess that means we're gonna throw Dad a bash then, huh?"

"Yes, we are. He wants a celebration, not a funeral."

"What else did he say, Mom?" my sister asks, wiping away another tear.

She turns toward Caroline with a hint of knowingness in her eyes—like she is about to reveal a secret. "He said he looks forward to seeing us all together again very soon, one way or another. He then kissed me good night and went to sleep."

27

Perfect Happiness

Radiate boundless love toward the entire world.

—**The Buddha**

"**H**ow are you feeling?" Judy asks, sitting down next to me at the kitchen table.

"Remarkably peaceful," I reply, setting my eulogy notes aside. "It's a little strange. I was expecting to feel a lot more anxious and emotional."

"You do appear to be relaxed," she agrees. "I'm feeling peaceful too. Maybe the course has something to do with this. Maybe it's finally starting to get through to us."

I think about the course. We're not even halfway through it, and already I have people telling me I've changed. I'm behaving differently at work. I'm no longer feeling as stressed as I used to. I've reconciled with my father and my siblings. Even my son, Kevin, noticed a difference when he arrived in town last night. He said I was a lot calmer and more relaxed than he expected.

"I think the course is helping," I reply. "Everything is starting to make a lot more sense to me now on a much deeper level."

"Yes, and it's comforting to know that your father isn't really dead, so to speak. He's simply moved on. The course is very clear about that."

I nod. "Well, we better be going soon. Are the kids ready?"

"Almost. I just checked on them, and they're getting dressed. I told them we have to leave in ten minutes and they promised they would be ready."

The venue we picked for my dad's service is a banquet room above Muldoon's, his favorite pub. Mom said he didn't want a fancy funeral. He just wanted to be cremated and his ashes spread among the rocks at Dowses Beach. My dad loved the ocean and the beach. Dowses was his favorite.

When we arrive at Muldoon's, there are already several people gathered there, waiting for us. Dad had a lot of friends. We exchange greetings and head up to the banquet hall to get prepared. One of my father's drinking buddies, Richard, is an ordained minister, and he has agreed to officiate the service. Like my dad, he is a bit gruff, but he has a heart of gold. And he has a great sense of humor.

I double-check my breast pocket to be sure the eulogy is there. It is. I take a deep breath and remind myself to relax. Despite my role as president of a large company, I do not like giving speeches, especially under these circumstances.

A stream of friends parades by our family on the way into the banquet hall, and we greet them with as much poise and grace as possible. My mother is handling the situation exceptionally well, which puts us all at more ease. I can't help but think about how tough this must be for her, despite her beliefs about eternal life.

Precisely at noon, we begin the service, and my dad's buddy, Reverend Richard, gets everyone laughing within the first five minutes. He knows my father well, and he has a wonderful way of sharing stories many of us have never heard. Clearly, behind my father's gruff exterior, there was a heart of gold. The banquet hall is packed.

I look over at my mom, and she is sitting peacefully, holding my brother's hand. This must be so hard for her. Even with her faith, she now faces life without her partner of nearly fifty years. I guess this is when true presence matters the most. She will have to take one day at a time.

As we get closer to eulogy time, my heart starts racing faster and faster. I'm immediately reminded of the Quick Coherence Meditation Technique, so I decide to use it. I sit quietly, focus on my heart center, and begin breathing very slowly to a count of four seconds in and four seconds out. I visualize myself breathing through my heart with appreciation, joy, and gratitude. I think about all the things I am grateful for, beginning with my father. Soon, I feel more relaxed and confident. I want to deliver my dad's eulogy with the most positive energy I can.

Before long, Reverend Richard gestures to me to come up and give the eulogy. I glance quickly at my mom, who looks at me with a loving twinkle in her eyes. Again, she has a knowingness about her—as if she understands something that no one else does.

I walk to the podium and clear my throat. "Greetings, everyone, and thank you for coming to celebrate the life and journey of my father, William MacDonald." I scan the faces in the crowd. There must be two hundred people here.

I continue. "I suppose it's moments like these that give us all an opportunity to pause in life to contemplate life. Why are we here? What purpose do we serve? Where did we come from, and where do we go? Are we here to learn lessons for soul development, and if so, what lessons? And from whom?" I stop and look at my mother.

She nods ever so slightly, as if to say, "Do it, Jack. Say it. Speak from the heart. People need to hear this."

I take another deep breath. "Maybe I can offer a little insight on a few of these questions. You see, I've really screwed things up from time to time, beginning with my father and my siblings. For some strange reason, I thought it was more important to be right than to be loved. As a result, I suffered, and in my suffering, I made things worse. Rather than atone for my criticisms and judgments, I let them form deep chasms between me and some of the people I love the most." Now I look right at my brother. "What a mistake. The more I built up defenses around what I thought was right, the more I fueled my own suffering.

"Friends and family, we are not here on this planet to criticize and condemn one another. We are here to forgive one another. And in forgiving one another, we are forgiving ourselves. We are setting ourselves free. The more we see past our differences to our Oneness, the freer we feel. There is nothing more important to humankind than positive, loving relationships and connectivity. Today, we remember this, and we celebrate it. We acknowledge that we are here to connect with one another. We are here to teach one another. We are here to pull together and help one another. And sometimes the best way to help someone is to not help them, to let them struggle, to let them figure things out for themselves, to be patient with them and allow them to stray a bit. My father was certainly masterful at this, and I was often too blind and stubborn to see it."

Suddenly, I catch a glimpse of Jordan and Nicole sitting in the back. They must have snuck in while I was talking with someone else or during Reverend Richard's sermon. Jordan winks. He certainly has let me struggle from time to time.

I continue. "Today, I honor and give thanks to my father for his love, his authenticity, his positive intentions, his discipline, and yes, even his harsh words. Even though we drifted apart for several years, I know my father was a man of love. He wanted the very best for me, for my mother, and for my siblings, and he worked very hard to provide it. Most of all, I give thanks for our forgiveness and reconciliation. You see, it was only a month ago that my father and I were not on speaking terms. Like I said, we drifted apart, and I was too proud and self-righteous to see my own ignorance. Thank God we made amends before he passed. Can you imagine the guilt and the grief one might live with by being so stubborn they can't say they're sorry?"

I see my sister wipe a tear from her eye and reach over to hold Judy's hand. Tears now start forming in my own eyes. "Here is another lesson I learned from my dad: Hell isn't some distant place we go to in the future if we're bad. It's a state of mind, just like heaven. It's a state of consciousness, here and now, a choice we make every day. And despite appearances, I was living in hell because of my own criticism and judgment. The more I condemned people and the more I convinced myself I was right, the more intense my suffering became. I honestly don't know if I would have learned this without my dad teaching me. Sometimes, I guess we learn things the hard way."

I wipe a tear away. *Get me through this, God. Please. Let me channel your Light*. I look up at the ceiling. "So, Dad, I know you're here in spirit, and I know you can hear me. Thank you for being exactly who you are and thank you for reconnecting with me after all these years. I can feel your love in my heart right now, and although it was a bit dramatic, you have your family back together again. Rest in peace, knowing we are now living in peace."

PART THIRTEEN

No One Can Fail Who Seeks to Reach the Truth

Out of difficulties grow miracles.

—Jean de La Bruyère

28

One with God

Resolutely train yourself to attain peace.

—**The Buddha**

Following the service, Muldoon's transforms from a temporary chapel into a bar. Toast after toast is made to my father, and I can feel his presence in the room. Thank God we made amends. I simply can't imagine the shame and guilt and grief I would be living with if I hadn't let go of my ego, ignorance, and stubbornness. Jordan was right. Sometimes we need to surrender to experience the real joy in life.

Suddenly, there is a tap on my shoulder. I turn around, and my brother is standing there. "You know, Jack, for a long time, I was really ticked at you," he says. "You said some things I had a hard time letting go of."

I'm about to jump in and start defending myself, but I stop and take a deep breath, reminding myself to relax and surrender. My brother is being honest with me. Let him talk. I nod my acceptance with empathy and compassion. I remember feeling the same way when my dad got defensive and talked down to me. Maybe it's best if I just shut up and listen.

He continues. "Until now, bro. The eulogy you gave Dad today really made me stop and think. Why am I carrying around all this emotional baggage? It's doing no one any good."

Again, I feel the ego trying to step in and take over. Now it wants credit for what I said. It wants to tell my brother that, again, I was right. I am the smart one. I know best. *You should listen to me more often.* It's like I have this new awareness of my false self, a voice inside me stirring up trouble. I remain quiet, dismiss the ego, and nod.

"So, thank you," he adds, reaching out his hand. "I really mean that."

I shake my brother's hand and then pull him in for a hug. My eyes immediately begin to fill with tears, and I feel an enormous heaviness lifted from my heart. I haven't felt this light and free in years. *Thank you, David. Thank you, Dad.*

"I have to tell you something," I finally whisper, slowly releasing the hug. "This might sound a bit crazy, but it's the truth. I didn't write the eulogy."

He steps back, looking puzzled. "What? Who did?"

I laugh. "Well, technically I wrote it. But what I'm really trying to say is that I think I had some spiritual guidance."

"You mean, like you channeled it or something? I've heard about people who do that."

"I guess you can call it that. I don't know. It was a very powerful experience, something I wasn't expecting."

Suddenly, Caroline walks up. "I saw you two hugging from across the room, and again, I want in. What's going on?'

I say nothing and give my sister a hug.

"Jack was just telling me how he channeled the eulogy," David explains. "It's no wonder I got the chills when I heard it."

"Oh my gosh," Caroline gasps. "I did too! Jack, I think you really touched people's hearts."

"Thanks, sis. I appreciate that."

"So, how did this happen?" my brother persists. "I want to hear the story."

I smile, reflecting on the experience and the fact that the three of us are now here together talking about it. "I guess I just let go."

My brother and sister look at each other and shrug. "C'mon, bro. We need more than that."

I take a pull of my beer. "Well, it's kind of hard to explain. I was sitting in Mom and Dad's study, trying to think of what to say, and a very powerful Presence seemed to enter the room. I couldn't see it or literally hear it, but it was very commanding and clear. I could feel it."

"Oh my gosh," my sister says. "Do you think it was Dad?"

"I don't know. I suppose, in retrospect, it could have been Dad."

"So, what did you do?" my brother asks.

"At first, I just sat there, wondering what to do. It was like an unwanted interruption at work, so I tried to brush it off. I had a eulogy to write. But the more I resisted and tried to focus, the more I was stumped."

Again, my brother and sister glance at each other. She is now beaming with excitement. "This is so cool."

"Well, it didn't feel so cool at the time," I reply. "In fact, it was kind of freaky. So, anyway, I finally gave up trying to write the eulogy myself. I remember saying, 'Okay, you tell me what to write.' And then ideas and words just started coming to me. It felt more like I was taking notes than writing something of my own."

David grins and looks at the beer in my hand. "And how many beers had you had at this point?"

"Zero at that point and one today, in honor of Dad," I reply, raising my mug in the air.

"Well, then, cheers to Dad!" he says, hoisting his mug.

Caroline joins in, clinking her glass with ours. "And here's to you, Jack," she says. "Thank you for your inspiring words, wherever they came from. You clearly connected with people at a whole new level—beginning with us. I feel very blessed."

29

They Know Not What They Do

Where ignorance is our master,
there is no possibility of real peace.

—His Holiness the Dalai Lama

The following morning, Kevin and Kathleen join Judy and me in our kitchen for breakfast. Kevin looks like he just rolled out of bed. He's still in his pajamas, and his hair seems to defy gravity. Kathleen looks like she's been up for an hour.

"You did a great job yesterday, Dad," Kevin says. "You really made me stop and think."

"Me too, Dad," Kathleen adds. "I'm proud of you."

I drink my coffee and smile at my children. "What did I make you think about?"

"Life, I guess," Kevin replies. "And how important it is to stay connected."

"And how important forgiveness is," Kathleen adds. "I see it at school all the time. People join cliques and keep people who are different out. The bullying is out of control."

Kevin nods. "It's no different in college. Everyone is just trying to fit in."

"I think it's pretty universal," Judy says. "We have cliques all over the hospital."

I suppose this is essentially what Jesus came to lead us away from. Cast off judgment and condemnation and learn to live in harmony and peace. This is what salvation and atonement are all about. We save the world by saving ourselves. And we do that by letting go of the ego and its thoughts of separation.

"Well, remember this if nothing else," I say. "True leadership is about pulling people together and harmonizing as one, not pitting people against one another."

"Is that what you're doing at TYPCO?" Kevin asks.

I laugh. "It's what I'm trying to do. Sometimes, it's easier said than done."

"I suppose that's what makes great leaders, Dad," Kathleen says. "I think about people like Abraham Lincoln and Martin Luther King Jr. They took great risks to pull people together."

"They sure did," I reply. "As did Jesus."

Kevin and Kathleen look at each other with surprise. They're not used to hearing talk of Jesus, or any other spiritual figure, at our kitchen table.

"Your father and I are taking a course together," Judy adds, as if reading their minds. "It's called A Course in Miracles. It's a course believed to be taught by Jesus."

Again, my children look at each other, this time with a hint of humor.

"Can I ask what you've been smoking?" Kevin chuckles. "I might want in on it."

We all laugh. That's Kevin, always clowning around. He's a lot like his uncle David.

Kathleen elbows her brother. "I think it sounds interesting. Can you tell us about it?"

For the next twenty minutes, Judy and I share insights from the course, observing different reactions from our children. Kathleen seems interested. Kevin has his doubts.

"So, basically, the course is about Jesus teaching us to think differently," he says with skepticism in his voice.

"That's right," Judy says. "It teaches us to think like Jesus, which is radically different than the way most of us have been conditioned to think."

"Well, that explains the change in your behavior, Dad," Kevin says boldly. "You've definitely been acting differently. You seem to be more relaxed and at peace."

I smile. "I'll take that as a compliment, Kevin. Thank you."

"It's true, Dad," Kathleen adds. "You've been acting a lot different lately. I like it."

"You too, Mom," Kevin says. "Both of you have a different feel about you. I'm happy for you."

"Can I take this course, Mom?" Kathleen asks. "It sounds like it might be another good way to eliminate some stress."

"That it is," Judy replies. "You can take it whenever you're ready. Just remember, it's a big commitment."

"Speaking of stress, I'm really struggling with career choices at school," Kevin says. "I honestly don't know what to do. On the one hand, I'm doing well in my business classes and my concentration in finance, but on the other hand, I don't really like it much."

I listen to my son and once again witness the ego surface for a say in the conversation. It wants to control Kevin and tell him what to do, like a know-it-all. This is what I've done for years with Kevin. In fact, I'm the primary reason he is studying business and finance. It's what I studied.

Suddenly, I remember something Jordan said to me. He challenged me to define my moments of bliss. What in life gets me excited? If I had all the money I needed, what would I do with my time? What do I love doing? What did I love doing as a child? When do I experience a sense of timelessness and peak productivity? These are all clues to identifying a person's moments of bliss, and this translates into our calling in life. When we are living our purpose, we are living with passion. And when we are living with passion, we blossom. Everything flows. Clearly, this is what Jordan appears to be doing with his life, and I'm beginning to understand why.

"What do you dream about, Kevin?" I ask, looking at my son. "If you could do anything, what would it be?"

He thinks about my question and then shrugs. "That's just it, Dad. I don't really know. I've always thought I have to follow the path you followed to become successful."

Instantly, my son's use of the word *become* hits me like a brick. I remember Jordan saying how words can reveal paradigms and deep-seated beliefs.

"Kevin, can I offer you a suggestion? It's something I learned from a very wise friend of mine. He said success isn't something you become. It's something you are, right here and right now. It's something you feel in the present moment. Whenever we think in terms of becoming, we are delaying success because we aren't tuning in to its vibration. Instead, we're tuning in to a frequency of scarcity and lack. That means success will always be out in front of us, and we will always feel like we're missing something."

He looks at me with a puzzled expression.

I continue. "Think in terms of energy. When we learn to adopt an energetic frequency of success, whatever that means for you, we're calling success into our lives. We're sending out a signal that returns to us in kind. This is called the law of attraction. We manifest what we dwell on. If we dwell on lack, we will continue to experience lack—in our careers, in our relationships, in our bank accounts, and in our lives. However, if we dwell on joy and prosperity and gratitude, joy and prosperity and gratitude will return to us. We don't have to work nearly as hard as we think we do."

He shakes his head with doubt. "Now you tell me. How am I supposed to do that, Dad, when all I feel is confusion and conflict and doubt? I have so much invested in college right now. What if I made the wrong choice?"

"Don't get me wrong, son. The key here is working smart, not hard. When we're working smart and everything is in alignment with what I like to call flow, life feels effortless. We're in harmony, balance, and alignment with who we really are."

"That's how I feel when I'm playing in the orchestra," Kathleen says. "It feels easy and fun. And it's timeless."

Kevin sits quietly, seemingly lost in thought.

Kathleen speaks again. "Maybe I can help, Kevin. I wrote a whole paper on this and got an A. Do what Dad suggested and think about your moments of bliss. You have a very creative mind. I remember your artwork when we were younger. You could draw anything. And you could visualize things in your mind better than anyone I know. Combine your creativity, your vision, and your intuition with your business training, and you can set the world on fire."

Judy and I look at each other with a hint of astonishment. Kevin isn't the only one who might set the world on fire.

I look back at Kevin, and I see a twinkle of light in his eyes.

"I have an idea," he says excitedly, getting up from the table, grabbing his phone and racing toward his room. "Thanks for the tips!"

PART FOURTEEN

I Am as God Created Me

If we could change ourselves, the tendencies in the world would also change. As a man changes his own nature, so does the attitude of the world change toward him. . . .
We need not wait to see what others do.

—**Gandhi**

30

The Cosmic Mirror

As I am, so are these. As are these, so am I.

—**The Buddha**

Something very different is going on at TYPCO. I can feel it in the air. When I return to the office, it appears to be quieter and more stable. People are less stressed and more engaging with one another. Is this my imagination? Are my associates putting on an act? Or is there something else at play here? I know my staff is sensitive to my father's passing, but this is different. I like it. It feels good.

I walk into my office and set my briefcase on the desk. Emily follows me.

"I cleared your calendar for the day, Jack," she says. "I figured you could use the time to catch up." I smile at her. "Besides, you didn't have anything too pressing."

"Thanks, Emily. That's very thoughtful." And different. Normally, she is loading me up like a camel crossing the Sahara. Of course, that's probably because I expect her to. Emily is an excellent assistant, and sometimes I think she can read me like a book.

I fix myself a cup of coffee and sit down at my conference table. Rather than go through my normal routine of emails and to-dos, I decide to sit quietly and contemplate things. I take a few deep breaths, close my eyes, and then begin a quiet meditation. I'm going to start today with a peaceful vibe. I missed my swim this morning, so this will have to do.

ACIM teaches that it is impossible to see two worlds. There is the ego world, and there is the world one sees with the vision of Christ. The world I've been seeing is obviously a world of chaos, drama, conflict, sin, guilt, attack, and defensiveness. The world I am seeing now is different. As I release the ego thought-system with all its flaws and insecurities, I see a world of perfect harmony and balance, a world impeccably designed for soul development and karmic resolution. It's like the universe is reflecting back whatever it is I'm looking for. If I see conflict and drama, it's because I'm asking for it, at least subconsciously. If I see harmony, peace, and grace, it's because I'm looking for it. How amazing! God is answering our prayers. We just don't know what we're praying for most of the time. We say we want something, but we subconsciously doubt we can have it. Our latent resistance is pushing it away.

I guess if there is one thing I want my children to know at this point in life it's that we reap what we sow. What could be more important than managing the energy we channel? Especially if we know that what we send we receive? If people knew that we are literally reaping what we're sowing, I imagine we might pay a lot more attention to what we think and believe and choose to dwell on. After all, these are critical seeds in the harvest of life.

Suddenly, I think of Joe and his upcoming kaizen event. I know he's been working with Jordan to prepare. Maybe I should go see how he is coming along. I sip my coffee and stand up, preparing for a little gemba.

Within seconds, Joe is standing at my door. I laugh to myself. Another synchronicity.

"Got a minute?" he asks.

"Yes, of course," I reply, returning to my seat at the conference table. "C'mon in and sit down."

"This won't take long," he says, still standing. "I just want to confirm that you can attend our daily briefings next week. It will really mean a lot to the team if you're present."

"I'll be there, Joe. You can count on it."

"Good," he says, smiling. "I think you might be blown away by some of the stuff the team is coming up with."

"Really? Any hints?"

He hesitates. "No, I don't think it would be right for me to say anything. I want the team to inform you. They've been working really hard at this."

Hmm, that's different. Normally, Joe wants all the credit for himself. "Okay, that's fine with me. How are things going with Jordan?"

"I have to tell you, Jack. The man is a genius. I don't know why I was so resistant at first. Maybe I felt a little threatened. Maybe I thought I could do it all myself. But if I've learned anything these past few weeks, it's that teamwork is the way to go. We have uncovered more hidden gems by going through this process than I ever imagined. It's no wonder our NPS is so low. Not only is the cart in front of the horse, but the horse is facing sideways with a confused look on its face. Our customer service reps are victims of a completely dysfunctional system."

"So, by bringing different stakeholders together to evaluate the system, the team can see the disconnects in the value stream, end to end?"

"Absolutely," he says without hesitation. He adds, "And we have anything but flow. We start and stop more than a car in rush-hour traffic."

Good visual. What an obvious pain our system is to navigate.

"And Jordan highly recommends we bring in a customer or two for the kaizen event," he adds. "So, we have two of our most important customers coming in to participate."

"That's exciting." I wonder who they are.

"And they're both detractors on the NPS. They're both very disappointed with our service, and they're telling us exactly why."

I nod.

He continues. "So, our strategy is to wow them not only by listening to their concerns but by acting on them immediately. What better proof of decisiveness and action is there than that?"

Normally, I would insist that Joe tell me who these customers are, and I would second-guess his approach. Instead, I say nothing. I choose to trust him.

"In fact, we've already worked ahead on some preliminary analysis, and we have a list of actions we can take during the kaizen event to accelerate improvement. You'll hear more about these changes next week."

"I'll be there, Joe. And let me just say, I'm really looking forward to it."

He smiles at me and shakes my hand. "It's a pleasure working for you, Jack. This is what I want to be doing with my career, and you've helped me see that. I'm not sure I could have honestly said this two months ago."

"Thanks, Joe. I think we're really starting to wake up and pull together as a team."

"We are. And it's very exciting."

Joe turns and heads for the door. He then stops and spins around. "Also, Jack, my prayers are with you and your family. I know this must be a tough time for you. I lost my father several years ago and not a day goes by that I don't think about him."

I bow my head. *Namaste*, Joe, I think. *The Christ in me recognizes and honors the Christ in you.*

31

Leading with Grace

The best effect of fine persons is felt after
we have left their presence.

—**Ralph Waldo Emerson**

When Joe leaves my office, I decide to continue my contemplation. Jordan suggested that contemplation can be just as helpful as meditation, if not more so. He said a lot of people struggle with meditation just like they struggle with listening. In effect, meditation and listening are very similar. When we meditate, we quiet the mind, we let go of resistance, and we listen. It is in stillness that the Holy Spirit speaks to us most clearly. When we contemplate, we simply weigh things without judgment. Rather than think in dualistic terms of right and wrong, good and bad, us and them, we consider all angles. Maybe there are other ways we can look at the situation. Maybe there are choices we haven't yet considered.

As I sit quietly, I contemplate my leadership style and how it has changed recently. In the past, my approach was very egocentric and fear-based. Everything was about right and wrong and "don't screw up." This led to a culture of division, anxiety, and stress. People protected themselves by covering their butts and keeping valuable information from me. I think my kids did the same thing at home.

This ego approach also valued titles, levels, classifications, and degrees. God knows how many job descriptions and grade levels we have at TYPCO. If you ask me, it's way too complex and confusing. We just keep adding and adding, complicating things. Maybe we should run a kaizen event on leaning out the ridiculous number of HR policies and programs we have.

And now that I think about it, we have the same pattern in accounting, procurement, scheduling, warehousing, distribution, and logistics. Again, this reminds me of that quote from E. F. Schumacher. "Any intelligent fool can make things bigger and more complex. It takes a touch of genius and a lot of courage to move in the opposite direction." I laugh to myself. I've been an intelligent fool—without even knowing it. No wonder Socrates claimed he knew nothing.

I suppose the good news is that I'm waking up. I'm beginning to see that the culture here at TYPCO reflects our senior management behavior, which begins with me. If I'm nervous and afraid, it sends a strong message out to my leadership team. And everyone else in the organization senses that tension and stress. Therefore, any significant culture change must begin with me. By recognizing and transcending the fear-based ego thought-system, I am sending out a very different vibration to everyone in the organization. We have nothing to fear. We are not separate. We are One. We are in this together. Anything we do to one another, we do to ourselves. Relax and enjoy the journey. Be mindful and present. Listen to your heart. Trust one another. The now is the only time that matters.

I decide to write down a few of these ideas. Maybe we can start using some of this in our leadership training. Come to think of it, we have nothing like this now. We're training our managers to be just like I used to be—to follow rules. We're not empowering them. We're imprisoning them with fear, along with everyone who works for them.

I begin by describing my traditional management style:

- Ego-based
- Fearful, anxious, doubtful, and insecure
- Independent
- Divisive
- Separates people and activities
- Competing and comparing
- Win-lose mind-set
- Command and control
- Push-oriented
- Argumentative; right-wrong dichotomy
- Aggressive; attack and defend
- Protect yourself; cover your butt
- Blame, point fingers, and make excuses
- Stubborn and resistant
- Never satisfied; always need more
- Proud; our side is better than your side
- Academic and intellectual
- Dramatic and cynical
- Rough and tough

Next, I contemplate some of the lessons in *ACIM* and how they have impacted my leadership style. What is it I'm doing differently now that is impacting our culture? I also think of Jordan and some of the qualities he has demonstrated so effectively. What does it mean to be miracle-minded?

- Spirit-based; in-Spirit
- Fearless, inspired, enthusiastic, eager, and faithful
- Interdependent
- United; think in terms of Oneness
- Integrates people and activities; connects
- Cooperating and sharing
- Win-win mind-set
- Influential, intriguing, and magnetic
- Pull-oriented
- Collaborative and innovative
- Peaceful and harmonious
- Honest and genuine; admits mistakes
- Forgiving, understanding, and compassionate
- Open and resilient
- Grateful and appreciative
- Humble; nothing to prove
- Wise and intelligent
- Mindful and present
- Graceful and confident

I finish my list and examine the two radically different styles side by side. I wonder how we can build these changes into our leadership development program. Will people think I'm nuts? This is so outside the typical corporate box. I decide to start with Georgia. She said she noticed a change in my behavior and wanted to learn more about it. Maybe it's time.

I get up from the table, grab my notes, and beckon to Emily. I want her to schedule an appointment with Georgia.

"What do you need, Jack?" Emily asks, walking into my office.

I think about what I'm doing. This is just one more example of complicating the simple. Emily and Georgia will go back and forth, checking calendars, to schedule something I can probably get done in five minutes.

"Never mind, Emily. I apologize. I'll take care of this myself." There is no time like the present. I head to Georgia's office.

PART FIFTEEN

By Grace I Am Released

We must cultivate our garden.

—**Voltaire**

32

Get Out of Your Own Way

A bad system will beat a good person every time.

—W. Edwards Deming

I catch Georgia at her desk, seemingly mesmerized by the computer screen in front of her. She probably has an inbox like mine, most of which is pure nonsense resulting from poor management. Rather than being proactive and eliminating a lot of inquiries and emails before they are sent, we have a culture of reactivity. We wait until things are on fire, and then we send in the fire brigade. Pure drama.

"Got a minute?" I ask, poking my head into her office.

"Sure," she says. "What's up?"

I take a page from Joe's book. "I'll be quick because I know you're busy. I just want to give you something to think about."

She nods curiously. "Okay."

"I want your opinion on mindfulness training for our managers. I've read about some other companies doing this, and I think it could be very beneficial here. I've even read that the British Parliament is doing it."

"You mean like yoga and stress management classes?"

"Yes. But even more than that. I want you to look into additional release techniques, like guided meditation and EFT."

"What's EFT?" she asks.

"It's a release method called Emotional Freedom Technique," I explain. "I want to help our managers eliminate stress, not just manage it."

She looks at me like I just turned green. "Eliminate it?"

"Yes," I say without hesitation. "I know it might sound a bit crazy, but I also know it works. I have personal experience with it."

"So, this is one of the things you've been doing to change your thinking. Some of us have been wondering what you're up to."

"Yes, and I want to build it into our leadership development program. I want TYPCO to be a place where people come to take their lives to a whole new level. We're not just a company that makes and sells stuff. We're a company that transforms people's lives."

I hand Georgia my notes. "Here are a few ideas I jotted down. This is the shift I want to see our leaders make—from ego management to miracle-minded management."

She glances at my notes, comparing the two very different styles. "Interesting," she says, looking up at me. "This is deep—and powerful."

"Well, it's far from perfect," I confess. "But, it's significantly better than what we're teaching our managers today. Obviously, we still need to emphasize the nuts and bolts of the business."

"Of course. But this gives people something positive they can take home and share with their families and friends. This will differentiate TYPCO from almost any company I know."

"That's why I'm calling it miracle-minded management. It's a radically unique way to see the world and interact with it."

"Is this what you've been doing, Jack?"

"Yes, Judy and I have been studying something called *A Course in Miracles*. It's completely changing our lives."

"Well, I can see that. Is the course something you want to include in our training?"

"No," I say quickly, having thought about this before. "We can refer to it and even recommend it, but I think the course should be voluntary for people—at least the timing of it."

"I see." She scribbles a note.

"But I want to incorporate a lot of the principles from the course into the training. You can see what I mean by looking at my lists. Obviously, we will have to explain what some of these differences mean."

She takes another look at my notes. "So, you want to keep this very practical and work-related, but you also want to teach our managers how to be more mindful and aware."

"Yes, and inspiring. I think the field of energy we can generate here with a team of enlightened managers will give us the greatest competitive advantage of all—something other companies will find hard to copy."

She smiles. "I'd phrase it this way: It will give us ideas that others will find hard to copy. I can already think of a few companies that are giving this a try, and when it comes to creativity and innovation, they're exploding with enthusiasm and ideas. With this new energy, we will all be able to see innovation that is uniquely ours."

"So, you'll help me put this together, please?"

"Consider it done," she replies eagerly. "This might be the most important thing I ever do here at TYPCO."

"Thanks, Georgia. I am eager to see what you come up with."
I turn for the door.

"And Jack," she adds as I leave her office, "I think you just
defined your legacy here. You will be remembered for this forever."

33

True Empowerment and Flow

> Only those who will risk going too far can possibly
> find out how far one can go.
>
> —T. S. Eliot

Jordan stands graciously at the entrance to our main training center, greeting people as they enter the room. Georgia arranged for him to come in and lead a one-day management workshop on mindfulness and culture change using some of the world's best practices. I wouldn't miss it for the world. Besides, my attendance also sends a strong message to anyone who might be feeling skeptical and resistant. We also timed this workshop to immediately precede the kaizen event briefings that Joe has scheduled for later this week—linking the two events together. I think this connection will be powerful. If all goes well, my management team will be intrigued to see what the kaizen team reveals throughout the week.

We have our top twenty executives and managers attending the training, probably half who genuinely want to be here. I insisted the training be mandatory simply because I knew it was the only way to avoid excuses and get everyone together. The kaizen briefings are mandatory as well.

Jordan opens the session right on time with a few provocative quotes from people like Albert Einstein, W. Edwards Deming, Martha Mead, and Peter Drucker, and then he moves quickly into a brainteasing exercise. He draws nine dots on a flipchart, forming what looks to be a square:

His instructions are simple. Using four straight lines, connect all nine dots. He also stipulates that you cannot lift your pen or pencil from the paper and you cannot back up. This should be easy enough. I quickly draw nine dots on my notepad and begin exploring options. Suddenly, it hits me. This isn't as simple as it looks. I laugh. Maybe Kathleen will have to help me with this one too. I stare at the image for a moment longer and then glance around the room. Others seem to be struggling with it as well. What an interesting strategy. He is gaining attention by giving these highly educated people a problem they cannot solve without letting go of misperceptions and limiting beliefs.

I return my attention to the nine dots. Jordan cautioned that we need to challenge our underlying assumptions and beliefs. We must look at things differently—from a variety of different angles. Kathleen solved the original puzzle by playing with it. She discovered that she had to challenge a paradigm she didn't even know she was in. Apparently, I need to do the same thing. What box am I in this time? Four straight lines. No lifting. No backing up. Hmm.

Jordan gives everyone a few minutes to solve the puzzle, which a few people do, but he insists that everyone keep their ideas and answers to themselves. No teamwork. At least not yet. He then informs us that he will reveal the answer later in the workshop if anyone still needs help. Apparently, he is going to keep us in suspense. Why am I not surprised?

Next, he leads the group through the first round of a simulation he designed that models a very common current-state scenario in business today (see page 210). There are six different departments, all isolated and narrow in focus. He gets one volunteer for each of the six roles, which require simple tasks like stapling paper, drawing lines, placing colored stickers inside images, and checking for mistakes. He has everyone else in the room play the role of an analyst, observing various elements of the process, including cycle times, customer service, and culture. Jordan gets into the game too. He plays the customer.

Once he has the game set up and everyone is ready to go, he places an order and starts a stopwatch he is wearing around his neck. He reminds us that time is a critical success factor in the value equation, so as the customer, he will be paying close attention to timely delivery. Originally, when he walked us through the round-one process, it appeared simple—like the brainteaser he gave us. The tasks are easy. Everyone is clear on what to do. But once he says, "Go," all hell breaks loose. Work suddenly starts piling up all over the place, like the massive inventory we have in our warehouse at TYPCO. People are frustrated and confused. Some people are overwhelmed with work, while others don't have enough to do. And Jordan isn't getting anything delivered on time. We finally hit the ten-minute mark, when the game is supposed to end, and he informs us that we need to work overtime since he has not yet received any deliveries. The room is aghast. Everyone recognizes this chaotic and confusing culture reflects our own current state at TYPCO. We all efficiently do our tasks, but there is no flow. There is no harmony and balance and coordination. The system is dysfunctional.

The simulation also has metrics and financials, so when we finish round one, we appear to be hopeless. We are late on deliveries to the customer. Inventory is piled up all over the place. We are swamped with defects. We lose money. And the customer is vividly upset.

"What I just did to you is what a lot of managers are unknowingly doing to their own people," Jordan says empathetically. "Like Deming said, and I'm paraphrasing here, put a good person in a bad system, and the bad system wins, no contest."

I see several heads nodding in agreement.

"So, being mindful begins with awareness," Jordan continues. "It's shifting from a mind-set of 'I think' to 'I know.' It's knowing the relationship between inputs and outputs, what we sow and what we reap. Some of you might remember this from eighth-grade algebra, even though a lot of people don't know how to apply it in life. It's called the transfer function, $Y=f(x)$. The Ys are the outputs, what we reap. The Xs are the inputs, what we sow. Y is a function of X. Everything happens for a reason. Stop and ask yourself, do you know the reason? And do you know the critical root causes to the problems you have? Do you understand the relationship between the Xs and the Ys?"

Georgia looks across the room at me and smiles. It appears she is already on board.

Jordan takes the next thirty minutes to lead my team through a methodology that helps facilitate rational problem-solving, emphasizing the word rational. We begin by defining the current state, exactly as it is now. We use tools like process maps and flow charts to visually clarify the steps and sequencing to get the job done. Like it or not, this is the way it is now. This reveals not only our current system but a key element of our culture as well—the way we do things around here. He adds that this is exactly what the kaizen team is doing in a large room down the hall. Tomorrow we will see the results.

Next, we add measures to the current-state process. How often do we make mistakes? What types of mistakes do we make? How long does it take to resolve issues? How long does it take to complete the process end to end? How many steps are there? How many of those steps are value-added? How many people are involved? How much does it cost to complete the process? What systems are we using to get the job done? What policies are we operating under? What measures do we have in place? The list goes on and on. Jordan has the group break out into teams to identify questions of their own relating to the simulation and then answer them. The data for round one is ugly. I can only imagine what the data on TYPCO will reveal tomorrow.

Jordan refers to this as the ugly baby syndrome. He cautions the team to be very careful with how they communicate their findings and opinions. Often, when we see something ugly, like a lousy design, and we say so to the owner of that process, it is interpreted as calling their baby ugly. This triggers a defensive and resistant response, and we get nowhere. Now we have two problems, the original problem and a new emotional problem.

"Let the facts and data speak for themselves," he suggests. "Paint a clear picture of the current state with accurate and influential information and let your audience draw their own conclusions. If it's ugly, they can see that for themselves."

This is how he facilitates kaizen events so effectively. He teaches the team how to define and measure a current-state process, and then he lets them report it to senior management in such a compelling way that we have no choice but to conclude we need to make immediate change. This creates a true sense of urgency.

Once we have the current state defined and measured, and everyone is aligned on what it is, we move into analysis. The key question here is why. Why are we getting the results we are getting? Why does it take as long as it does? Why are we making mistakes? What are the root causes? This is where we use tools like the Five Whys to get down to where the real action is, the strategic leverage points. In the case of the simulation, it is the design of the process, along with a few other things like policy, tooling, and measurement. People can be totally motivated and inspired to do excellent work, but they will fail because the process is dysfunctional. This is exactly what we have going on with our customer service. We have good people in a lousy system.

Next, the real fun begins. Once Jordan has explained how important it is to be mindful of the current state, including performance measures and root causes, he says it's time to get creative.

"There are multiple solutions to every problem," he suggests. "And there is no problem without a solution. Think of this like two sides to the same coin. One does not exist without the other."

I see a few people scribbling notes. The energy in the room feels good. Jordan then offers a few creative problem-solving tips, like silent brainstorming and something known as the third right answer. He says he will explain each in just a moment. He wants to remind us about kaizen and making good change. He tells us that things are not perfect now, so don't worry about making them perfect. Just make things better—fast!

We can start by generating dozens of clever ideas within fifteen minutes using silent brainstorming. Simply, everyone writes down as many ideas as possible on sticky notes, one idea per sticky. No judgment is allowed during this collection phase. Next, we categorize the ideas on a wall, grouping each idea with like ideas. For example, one grouping might be labeled design. Another might be labeled policy, another training, measurement, tooling. Chances are, there is no one single solution to the problem. So, rather than debate over option A and option B, we explore multiple options in harmony with one another, or the third right answer. This stimulates creativity and openness, a key factor in mindfulness. We want to keep the mind open.

Jordan then breaks the group into teams of five to six people, and he has them "compete" for the best performance in another round of the simulation. Each team must come up with kaizens, or good changes, and demonstrate them in front of one another. He gives them ninety minutes to come up with a solution the whole room agrees on. This fills the room with enthusiasm and excitement. It also sets the stage for the teams to learn from one another during the demos.

Jordan walks over and sits down next to me in the back of the room. "Since you've seen this exercise before, Jack, may I suggest you quietly listen to the dialogues taking place among the teams. It can be quite revealing. You'll hear all kinds of assumptions surfacing and being debated without mindfulness and awareness."

"This is like the exercise you showed me with the six circles, right? People are in a box, and they don't know it."

"Yes, that's exactly right." He then looks down at the nine dots scribbled on my notepad, that puzzle still unresolved. "And being mindful inside a box is not the same as being mindful of the box."

I catch his glance and suddenly feel a flash of insight. It's like a

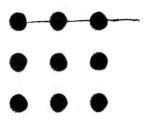

light bulb went on inside my head. The box! The paradigm! Aha! I have to think outside the box. I return my attention to the nine dots on my notepad and grab my pen. I start by drawing one line and then pause.

"You mean like this?"

Jordan smiles. "That's interesting. What's next?"

I draw a second line, keeping my pen on the paper.

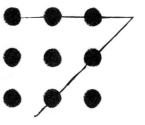

"Now that's thinking outside the box." He chuckles. "You have two lines left."

I finish up the exercise, feeling very accomplished. "How's this?"

"Brilliant," he says. "You did it. Now, observe the teams in this room and pay close attention to the paradigms, or boxes, blocking their visions. I think you will find it quite enlightening—especially when they reveal their solutions to one another."

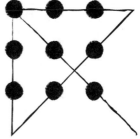

"I will," I say standing to do a little gemba. "Thank you."

"Don't mention it," he says. "Oh, and by the way . . . you can complete the nine-dot exercise with only three straight lines."

I shake my head. "Are you kidding me?"

"Think about it." He laughs. "And when you figure that out, try completing it with only one straight line."

The Lean Sigma Game

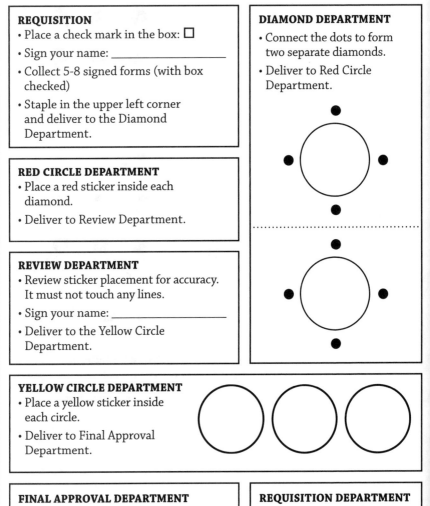

REQUISITION
- Place a check mark in the box: ☐
- Sign your name: _____
- Collect 5-8 signed forms (with box checked)
- Staple in the upper left corner and deliver to the Diamond Department.

RED CIRCLE DEPARTMENT
- Place a red sticker inside each diamond.
- Deliver to Review Department.

REVIEW DEPARTMENT
- Review sticker placement for accuracy. It must not touch any lines.
- Sign your name: _____
- Deliver to the Yellow Circle Department.

DIAMOND DEPARTMENT
- Connect the dots to form two separate diamonds.
- Deliver to Red Circle Department.

YELLOW CIRCLE DEPARTMENT
- Place a yellow sticker inside each circle.
- Deliver to Final Approval Department.

FINAL APPROVAL DEPARTMENT
Review sticker placement for accuracy. The outer circle must be completely visible.
- Sign your name: _____
- Return to the Requisition Department.

REQUISITION DEPARTMENT
- Separate completed forms.
- Collect eight completed forms.
- Deliver eight forms to the customer.

PART SIXTEEN

Let Me Not See Myself as Limited

Imagination is everything.
It is the preview of life's coming attractions.

—Albert Einstein

34

Answer Your Calling

Nothing can resist the human will that will stake
even its existence on a stated purpose.

—Benjamin Disraeli

When I get home, Judy is standing in the kitchen with a crafty grin on her face.

"Kevin wants you to call him when you get a chance," she says. It looks like she knows something she isn't going tell me.

"Is everything okay?" I ask, setting my briefcase on the kitchen table and kissing her.

"Isn't that a matter of perspective?" she teases, reflecting insights from *ACIM*.

"Yeah, I guess it is. And from the sounds of it, you aren't going to tell me anything."

"Call him," she says, offering me a beer with an insinuating smile. "He has interesting news."

I look at the beer and then at Judy. I suppose this could mean anything. "Thanks, but I think I'll have a sparkling water tonight instead. I've lost ten pounds since we went to that first *ACIM* meeting, and I want to lose ten more."

Judy swaps the beer for a water. "What? You think I haven't noticed?"

It does feel good. I feel more energy. I'm sleeping better. I'm more relaxed. My clothes aren't as tight. And all I'm really doing is eating more whole foods, swimming a few times a week, starting my day with a highly nutritious smoothie, and meditating. I suppose I'm just being more mindful and aware of the choices I'm making.

I walk into the living room and call Kevin. He answers on the second ring. This is different. Usually, I get his voicemail.

He's laughing. "Hey, Dad, I take it you talked to Mom." I can hear several people and music in the background.

"Yes, I did," I reply curiously, sitting down. "But she told me nothing. What's up?"

He pauses for a moment as if to take a deep breath. Then I hear his reply: "I think I found my passion. I know what I want to do with my career, at least for now." Silence again, which I take as provoking a response.

"Okay," I say, hooked. "What is it?"

"Well, remember how you suggested I think about my moments of bliss and activities that seem timeless and highly productive?"

"Yeah, I remember."

"And remember what Kathleen said about combining my creativity and my intuition and my sense of adventure with my business training?"

"Yes, I remember that as well." I feel like I'm talking to Jordan. *Just come out with it, son.*

"And you know how I've been working part-time at a microbrewery?" he hints.

I look at Judy, who is grinning at me from across the room. "Yes, I recall you telling me that."

"And you know how you often say we have to connect the dots in life—that everything is connected energetically?"

How can I argue with that? I can feel his energy and enthusiasm through the phone.

"Well, I want to make beer for a living. I want to run a brewery."

I sit silently, contemplating his revelation. He has no doubt given this a lot of thought. I can feel his passion and excitement, despite being hundreds of miles apart. And I know it takes courage for him to tell me this. It's very different in terms of career paths than what I have done. And it's very different than what he believes I expect from him. He is bucking the system, so to speak. He is thinking outside the box, or the bottle. He's being a rebel. And he loves it!

"You really love this idea, don't you, Kevin," I say empathically.

"Yes, I do, Dad. And it fits my personality profile. I'm a creative, entrepreneurial type. I don't belong in a traditional business setting, especially not in corporate finance. I might be good at numbers, but I don't like the idea of sitting at a desk. It's not the right fit for me."

I nod in agreement as if he can see me.

"And I've already learned so much here at the brewery," he continues. "The master brewer really likes me, and he's been showing me the ropes. He also respects my opinion on business matters, so we're already brainstorming franchising and merchandising opportunities."

"That's interesting," I say. "I had no idea."

"Well, I never put this together until recently," he admits. "And I never really considered it an option, even though it was right in front of me."

I think about my learnings over these past few months and the whole idea of miracle-minded management. How often are we staring right at an answer and we can't see it?

"And I was afraid to talk to you about the idea of entrepreneurship because I thought you would rather see me follow a more stable and predictable path—like you did."

I take a deep gulp, without a drink. How open and mindful have I been? My own son was afraid to talk to me about things outside my box.

"Have you reviewed the brewery's business plan?" I ask curiously, trying to align with Kevin.

He laughs. "Dad, that's one of the reasons Max wants to bring me in full-time when I graduate. He hardly has a business plan. This is a guy who just loves making good beer and serving people. He's not academic. That's where I can add value. This place can really take off with a well-written business plan, something we can put in front of serious investors and marketers."

My son's passion is now getting me excited. Maybe I should look at investing in this company. I love microbeers, and they're obviously taking off all over the country. "What's the name of this place, anyway?"

"Maximum's Brewery," he answers proudly. "I helped Max come up with the name."

I laugh. Pretty clever. "Can I call it Mac's for short?" I ask, referring to my son's nickname.

My son laughs, connecting the dots. "Maybe that's another good sign. Next time you come visit me, I want you to see this place. You'll love Max, and you'll love this place. Talk about a great vibe."

"You're there now?" I ask, feeling envious.

"Yeah," he replies. "I'm working. It's happy hour."

"Well, I'm happy for you, Kevin. Thanks for sharing this with me."

"One more thing, Dad," he adds, before hanging up. "You know how you often talk about flow?"

"Yeah."

"Well, I'm in flow. And it feels great!"

"Yes, you are, Kevin. Your energy speaks for itself."

35

The Third Right Answer

Any fool can make a rule—and every fool will mind it.
—**Henry David Thoreau**

"**C**an I ask you something, Jordan?" I say, looking at him across the table. We're back in our favorite French café.

"You just did," he teases with a smirk, sipping his tea.

I laugh, shaking my head. "Okay, then another question . . . What do you know about microbreweries?"

"They're hot right now," he replies without hesitation. "They're popping up all over the country. Why do you ask?"

I share my recent conversation with Kevin, and Jordan summarizes it by saying he thinks my son found a clever third right answer. "He's connecting the dots," he concludes. "That's quite a gift."

"You mean, he's connecting things that a lot of people might assume are unrelated," I surmise. "Like beer and finance?"

"Exactly," he says enthusiastically. "Like you're doing with miracles and management. We've talked about this before. Everything in the universe is connected. Creativity is all about recognizing this—seeing patterns, needs, opportunities, and solutions and putting it all together."

"That's what we're trying to do more of at TYPCO—think more like innovators and entrepreneurs."

"Yes, you are. You can see it with your kaizen events. You're pulling things together by connecting dots and improving flow. You're bringing entrepreneurial spirit back into a tired old business with antiquated thinking."

I nod in appreciation. Our recent kaizen event didn't just change several processes and activities. It changed people's minds!

"And flow isn't just about material flow, information flow, and cash flow," Jordan says. "It's about human flow. It's about boosting creativity, confidence, motivation, and performance by transcending fear and doubt. This is what a lot of high-performing athletes call the zone."

"I hear you. That seems to be where Kevin is right now. He's in the zone."

"Well, if you ask me, you should be very happy and grateful for that. What a wonderful feeling for any parent to have."

I start to push back with my doubts about Kevin's income stability and health benefits, and then I recognize it is ego that wants to push back. My ego. Kevin seems to have let that go. He's inspired. He's in-Spirit. He's ready to take on the world, and I'm worrying about how he's going to pay his rent. I quietly dismiss the ego.

"I am happy for him," I hear myself say, half-wondering if I mean it. The ego doesn't let up easily.

"But?" Jordan pokes, as if reading my mind.

"I get it," I reply. "You always told me to be careful with the word but. It usually precedes an excuse or form of resistance."

"And it's a word the ego loves to use," Jordan says. "Whenever you find yourself wanting to say it, try stopping and replacing it with the word *and*."

I think about this subtle difference in word choice. The word *but* reveals an either-or mentality, a very common paradigm. This or that. Yeah, but. Option A is good, but option B is better. I'd love to help, but I can't. You can win, but then someone must lose. The word *and* is more inclusive and expansive. It challenges us to think outside the but box.

"So, maybe what I should be thinking right now is I'm happy for my son, and there are things I can do to help him, beginning with letting go of my worries and concerns."

"Precisely," Jordan replies. "How are your worries and concerns going to help anything? Or anyone? Remember, they're coming from the ego thought-system."

I contemplate this.

"But what about the risks and the instability?" I challenge, immediately recognizing my use of the word *but*. "Excuse me. I meant to say, *and* what about the risks and the instability? Isn't it wise to consider this?"

Jordan laughs. "Use FMEA for that," he says without hesitation, referring to another problem-solving tool he taught us at TYPCO. Failure Mode and Effect Analysis is a risk-mitigation tool we use by considering all the things that can go wrong with an idea or a solution and then coming up with countermeasures to make sure they never happen.

I want to kick myself. How is it I don't remember this stuff? It seems second nature to Jordan. He lives it. I still think of it as some tool we use in isolated circumstances at work, like the Five Whys.

"So, you're suggesting I use FMEA with my son to help him mitigate some of the risks he is taking?"

"Sure, why not? Plus, it will help you gain confidence in him. Rather than second-guess and resist what your son is doing with a *but* mentality, you will align and flow with him. Combine your immense experience and wisdom with his hungry mind and motivation, as well as his need for support, and you will flow together. You will synergize. This is what the power of teamwork is all about. Add one plus one and get something greater than two."

I think about this. "I suppose it will give him more confidence too. Knowing he has my genuine support."

"Yes, it will. It will help him see past his own doubts. What better way to help your son than that? Plus, you'll be giving him a tool he can use to mitigate risk at the brewery. It's win-win."

As Jordan says this, I can't help but think about his loss. His only child. The son he never got the chance to do this with.

PART SEVENTEEN

I Can Be Hurt by Nothing but My Thoughts

Meditate . . . do not delay, lest you later regret it.

—**The Buddha**

36

Fear or Faith?

> Go put your creed into your deed.
>
> —**Ralph Waldo Emerson**

When I arrive on campus to visit Kevin, I feel an energy and an exuberance I seem to have forgotten. There is excitement in the air. Students are hustling about, connecting with one another, learning, growing, exploring, and expressing themselves. This is what I want more of at TYPCO. We're making progress, and I'm happy about that. Now it's time to hit the accelerator. Maybe I can pick up a few more tips while I'm here.

I decided to visit Kevin in person rather than talk by phone. Jordan encouraged it, and Judy agreed, even though she elected to stay home. My primary interest is to learn more about his career intentions and offer any help I can. I also want to check out this brewery he's talking about. Who knows what I might learn? It's time for some more gemba.

While he is still in class, I decide to walk around the campus and get some fresh air. This is another new habit of mine. I am walking more, combining it with my meditations and contemplations. I find they go well together.

Kevin asked me to meet him in the lobby of the business school, and we could go from there. I get to the building a little early, so I take a few minutes to walk the halls and glance at some of the posters and postings on the wall. The place is flooded with information. Companies are coming from all over the country to interview and recruit students. Strangely, I do not see TYPCO listed anywhere, even though we have several openings, including one in accounting. I will have to ask Georgia about this. I just hope we're not falling into the same trap a lot of other companies are, relying solely on technology and social media to hire top talent. That seems to take forever, and half our new hires leave within two years. Whatever happened to face-to-face recruiting and real-time hiring?

Kevin greets me with a hug in the lobby, introduces me to one of his classmates, and we head to Maximum's Brewery. His buddy, Larry, turns out to be an accounting major, and Kevin tells me he is a real whiz kid. On our walk to the pub, which is in the neighborhood, I get a chance to learn more about Larry and his aspirations. Like me, he wants a steady job with a large company where he can pursue his CPA and MBA. Ultimately, he wants to be a senior executive like his mother.

As I listen to his story, I can't help but wonder why we aren't hiring this kid. I don't need keywords, filters, and piles of applications to sort out what I'm looking for. I want this kid. He is super impressive.

"Have you decided where you're going to work when you graduate, Larry?" I ask.

"Not yet, Mr. MacDonald," he replies. "I'm still interviewing and sorting things out."

"Do you have any offers?"

"I have one. And I have second interviews scheduled next week with two other companies. Hopefully, I can lock something in by the end of the month."

"What about TYPCO?" I try to restrain myself, but I cannot. "Have you considered coming to work for us?"

Larry looks at Kevin and appears to want to avoid the question.

"Go ahead," my son says, poking him in the arm. "My dad should probably hear this." Evidently, Kevin has informed Larry of my role at TYPCO.

I look curiously at Larry. "Go ahead, Larry. Talk to me."

He shrugs. "I put an application in about six weeks ago, and I haven't heard back yet."

I immediately feel my blood pressure rising. *Breathe slow and deep, Jack. Relax. This is just one more opportunity in disguise. Let the situation teach you.*

"And he's followed up twice, Dad," Kevin adds, throwing a little fuel on the fire. "Still no response. And it's for a position in your business unit."

I can only think of one thing to say. "Larry, I don't know if Kevin has shared this with you, but we're shaking things up at TYPCO. And what you just described is unacceptable to me. I apologize on behalf of the company."

"It's okay, Mr. MacDonald." He sighs. "It's not that unusual. Some companies never respond."

I am about to declare war on our HR department when I suddenly stop. That's just another form of blaming and finger-pointing. It doesn't solve anything. What would a miracle-minded manager do, especially one in my position?

"I'll tell you what, Larry. If you're still interested in coming to TYPCO and you have the guts and motivation to help change things, I'll schedule you right now for first, second, and third interviews all in the same day. Furthermore, I'll commit to giving you an answer one way or the other by the end of that same day, assuming you can provide good references."

"Wow," Larry gasps. "That's decisive."

"That's my dad," Kevin says with a smile. "And he means it."

"I'm sure he does," Larry says with admiration. "I'm in, Mr. MacDonald. Let's do it! I'll take the interviews."

"And by the way, Dad," Kevin says, "Larry has impeccable references. TYPCO would be missing out big-time on a guy like this."

We walk in silence while I contemplate some more changes we need to make at TYPCO. I hardly notice when Kevin suddenly stops and says, "This is it, Dad. Welcome to Maximum's!"

Had he not said something, I think I probably would have walked right by. From the outside, the place looks like a deserted warehouse, which is apparently what it was not long ago. There are a few holes in the siding, a crack in the one window that is visible, and an old wooden door that looks like something out of the eighteenth century.

Kevin seems to read my face. "Don't judge a book by its cover, Dad. We all know it needs work, and I'm going to find the capital to do it. Just wait until you taste the beer."

I decide to keep my judgments to myself. Better yet, I commit to keeping an open mind and contemplating the possibilities. When Kevin swings open the heavy door and we walk in, it feels like we just morphed time and space. The place is packed with students and young professionals, buzzing with energy and spirit. Kevin is treated like a rock star, getting high fives from his patrons and hugs from several young ladies. Max comes over and introduces himself, handing me a draft he says he picked out just for me. He looks like a character out of a Paul Bunyan book: tall, thick, with a bald head and a long goatee.

"Kevin tells me you like a good barrel-aged stout," he says, beaming with pride. "Let me know what you think of this one."

I drink my beer as Max disappears and then look at Kevin. "Mmm, I've never tasted anything quite like this. Be sure to put this in your business plan. You'll get plenty of funding."

"Just wait, Dad. We have twelve different brews right now, and we're working on three more. We're also experimenting with some distilling."

"How old is this place?" I ask, taking another sip of my stout.

"Well, the building is ancient," Kevin replies. "That's obvious. The brewery itself is eight years old, started by Max in his garage. We moved here a year ago."

"And how long have you been involved?" I ask while thinking I should know this.

"Two years," he says. "I met Max through a couple of friends and started helping him in his garage. We also helped him find this warehouse and move here."

I look at Larry. "Are you a part of this brew club?"

He doesn't hesitate. "I am, Mr. MacDonald. I work here part-time as well."

I nod and smile. The enthusiasm is contagious. This is what we need more of at TYPCO. Talk about passion and energy. These guys are excited about what they're doing even though they're working out of a dungeon.

"Dad, when it's not so busy, I want you to spend some time with Max. I think it's a win-win opportunity."

"How so?" I ask, sensing a sales pitch.

"You'll see," he replies. "Max is a pretty incredible guy. We just need some mature guidance to grow this business. I was thinking that with your experience, maybe you could be like an advisor to us."

I consider the possibility and all the help Jordan has given me. I also think about the connection I can build with my son around this idea. Rather than resist, maybe I need to let go and let flow.

"Sure, son. Let's set it up. I love the idea of win-win, and you know I like a good beer when I taste it."

Kevin grins ear to ear and gives me a hug. Already, I'm feeling a connection with my son I haven't felt in years.

37

Emergence

The purpose of our lives is to be happy.

—**His Holiness the Dalai Lama**

On the way home from my visit with Kevin, I stop and sit quietly for a while to contemplate life. A flower doesn't try to bloom. It just does. Growing and blooming and emerging as a flower are its essence. The same is true for an acorn and a child. We're all here for a reason. We're all here to emerge as the sacred beings we are. All we really need to do is get out of our own way.

Kevin is developing into quite a young man. He has explored different avenues, including the one I chose to take as a career, and he has decided to take a different path. I remember the same itch when I was his age. I thought it might be fun and exciting to build something of my own. I simply talked myself out of it, with the help of my dad. There were a lot of "yeah, buts" involved. Yeah, but it isn't practical. Yeah, but there are too many risks. Yeah, but you're never going to make any money doing that. Yeah, but how are you going to support a family without a steady income? Yeah, but what about health benefits?

In retrospect, I know my dad was trying to help me from the paradigm he was in. He valued security and predictability. He valued hard work. In fact, he was insistent. At the time, he made a lot of sense, and I followed his lead, even though deep down I harbored some hostility. *Why can't I decide what I want to do? Why do I always have to do what you tell me?*

Now that I'm becoming more aware of what is really going on in the world energetically, I know I need to release these negative thoughts and hostilities. They do nothing but attract more negativity into my life and weigh me down. And they almost destroyed my relationship with my dad. I will not let that happen with my son. At least he has the courage to stand up to me and tell me what he really wants. Maybe this is another test for me, a synchronicity designed to awaken me further.

Life has really changed since I started *ACIM*. Or maybe it hasn't, and it just seems to have changed because of my shift in perception. Before *ACIM*, everything seemed separate and independent. Life was chaotic, dramatic, and stressful because of all the ups and downs and unfortunate things happening.

Now, life appears more like a symphony with perfect timing, harmony, and balance. Of course it has its ups and downs, but this is what gives us contrast. Nature points this out to those who pay attention. We have day and night. We have summer and winter. We have life and death. We have continuous flow and emergence. An oak tree doesn't work hard to grow tall and bear acorns. It just does. Everything is flowing and happening for a reason. If things don't work out as we plan, and we learn something new in the process, how can we call this a failure? It's simply an element of growth.

Who knows what will happen with Kevin and his beer venture? The outcomes aren't the only things that matter. The journey matters. The moment-to-moment experiences and feelings matter. Come to think of it, I haven't seen Kevin this happy and excited since he was a kid. A memory surfaces from long ago. One of his favorite things to do was sell lemonade on the Fourth of July as the parade went by. Who knows, maybe he'll come up with a lemonade beer?

Max is passionate and excited too. My chat with him was short yet very compelling. He dropped out of college to start brewing because he loved it, he was good at it, and he had a vision for using his skills to bring people together in community. He said he loved the whole concept of a pub, where people gather to talk and share stories, especially in this techno age of smartphones and impersonal communication. I have to say, he may not have finished college, but he is one sharp guy.

I also got a look at the preliminary business plan. It needs some polish, but the main components are there. They have a solid executive summary, crystallizing their vision, overall strategy, and reason for being. The marketing and financing plans need work, which they know, and the organization and operations plans are solid, at least for now. Kevin and Larry are working on the finance plan, and they have even used it as a case study in one of their classes. Now, from what they tell me, they have one of their finance professors interested in the business, and he is giving them some tips on how to raise capital. What great real-life experience! The more I get to know Larry, the more I like him.

They have some smart ideas on how to market some of their bestselling brews to local retailers, restaurants, and bars. They have already acquired equipment for canning and bottling as part of their operations plan, and they are leveraging several college students to help sell the brand in the local area. I have to say, I am genuinely impressed, despite first appearances.

I agreed to serve as an adjunct board member and advisor, and I'm even considering making a financial investment in the company. I just want to talk to Judy about it. Despite a few holes in the finance plan, I see some huge upside potential, and this might be a good way for us to diversify our portfolio.

Suddenly, my mind jumps to the practice of gemba, getting off our butts to go see what is really going on. I've been using the technique more and more at TYPCO, and now I see its value in parenting. Rather than simply looking at reports and getting summary updates, I am getting to see people in action and feel the energy of the culture. Honestly, that's why I said yes to serving as an advisor and possibly making an investment. On paper, there is no way I would have given this company my attention. In general, I'm very conservative with my money, and spontaneity is not a characteristic of my personality type. And I'm not doing this to give my son a handout. We both know better than that. This is a bona fide business opportunity. I can feel it. There is an energetic attraction.

PART EIGHTEEN

Fear Binds the World; Forgiveness Sets It Free

The more you are motivated by love,
the more fearless and free your action will be.
—His Holiness the Dalai Lama

38

Karma

We can never obtain peace in the outer world until we
make peace with ourselves.

—His Holiness the Dalai Lama

The harborside restaurant Jordan picked for dinner is beautiful. Boats are coming and going from the marina, reggae music is playing in the distance, and it's a warm autumn evening, so we choose a table outside. Jordan selects a nice bottle of champagne. While Nicole and Judy freshen up inside, we take a few minutes to catch up on business.

"We're gaining momentum at TYPCO," I say, taking in the salt air. "You really got a lot of people's attention with the mindfulness workshop and that first kaizen event. Thank you!"

"Thank you," he volleys back. "You're the one leading the charge. I'm simply at your service."

"When Nicole and Judy get back, I want to talk to you more about synchronicity, miracles, and blessings in disguise," I continue. "I know Judy does too."

He has a hint of knowingness in his eyes. "You're experiencing more and more of these holy instances?"

"Seems like every day now. Sometimes, several times a day. I'm not sure what to make of it."

He leans forward, like a coach leaning into a huddle. "Don't try too hard to analyze it or figure it out. You're wasting your time, and it doesn't matter. I went through the same thing. I wanted to know everything that was going on and why. Maybe it was my academic training or my business experience. Doesn't matter. It's just another form of resistance—an ego distraction."

"So, that's another thing I have to let go of—the tendency to want to know everything and figure everything out?"

"It is," Jordan says. "I had to do the same thing, and when I did, it was very freeing. There's a peace that comes with accepting uncertainty."

"Ha! I'm going to have to work on that."

"Don't work on it," he suggests, leaning back. "Work implies it's going to take time and effort. Simply let it go. Use release techniques to eliminate the perceived need. Remember, the need isn't real. It's only in your mind."

"Let go of what?" Judy asks, returning to the table with Nicole. "This sounds like something I need to hear."

The ladies sit down, and we catch them up on our conversation. Nicole suggests EFT as a practical technique for letting go of these perceived needs and says she has used it herself on this very tendency.

"I used to think I needed to know everything," she reveals. "I don't know if this was a control issue or a matter of subconscious insecurity or a hidden desire to be accepted, but I can say this. It isn't healthy. It weighs us down. It causes unnecessary stress. It's the ego subtly working against us."

Our champagne arrives, and we toast to freedom. Not freedom in a national or political or religious kind of way, but freedom from fear and doubt and insecurity and stress. Freedom from our own limiting beliefs. Freedom from things we think we need that we don't. True, pure freedom.

"Well, if there's one thing I'm learning from the course, it's the relationship between forgiveness and freedom," Judy says. "I can see it in myself, and I can see it in Jack. We simply aren't who we thought we were."

"Imagine what the world will be like when we all awaken to this truth," Nicole says with a smile. "Jesus isn't the second coming. We are. Each one of us. And all of us together."

Just as Nicole says this, a pair of mourning doves land on the roping near our table. Normally, I would have shooed them away, like I do seagulls. But this time I just look at them. We all do. It's like we all sense that this is more than a coincidence. It's another synchronicity. It's a cosmic message. Yes, we are the second coming, all of us together. There is no us-them dichotomy. We're all one with God and in God. We are the Christ. What better than a pair of doves to confirm this?

"How come you never talk about the course in your work, Jordan?" I ask.

He smiles thoughtfully and sips his champagne. "Talk is cheap, Jack. You know that. I simply think it's more effective to quietly walk the talk, to model the thinking and the behavior we desire."

"I guess you're right. There certainly are plenty of people out doing the opposite—saying one thing and doing something different. The next thing you know, they're eating their own words."

"That's karma for you," Nicole offers. "What goes around comes around."

Judy sits up straighter. "I always wondered about karma," she says. "I don't really know much about it, but I hear it referenced more and more. Can you help me understand it better?"

Nicole smiles. "Sure, I can try. Karma is essentially a universal law of harmony, balance, and perfect justice. All debts get paid, one way or another, so to speak. No exceptions." Nicole looks from Judy to me. "Think of it this way. Judgment Day isn't an event in the future at the Pearly Gates. It's an ongoing phenomenon. It's happening every moment of every day."

"So, if I'm kind and generous to someone, they will be kind and generous to me?" Judy asks, somewhat skeptically. I have similar doubts.

"Not necessarily," Nicole explains. "Karma is more universal than that. Since we are all connected as One, whatever you sow you will reap—somehow. In this case, it may not be the person you were kind and generous to who responds in kind. In fact, they may run off and you will never see them again. But your kindness and generosity do not go unnoticed. Kindness and generosity will come back to you from somewhere, sometime, and somehow. Everything balances out."

"That's interesting," I say. "I never thought of it that way."

"Neither did I," adds Judy.

"You're not alone," Nicole says softly. "That's because the ego looks at it differently. I help you out, so you help me out. It's a one-on-one relationship based on separation. In fact, if you're generous with someone and they run off on you and you hold a grudge, you're now sowing different seeds. Your vibration has shifted from one of kindness and generosity to one of hostility and condemnation."

Judy nods. "So, this is why forgiveness is so important. By forgiving people who have hurt us in some way, and maintaining a positive, healthy, loving attitude, we remain open to receiving blessings from somewhere else. It doesn't have to come directly from the person we helped."

"That's right. We always have a choice on how we respond. And remember, we all have karma to deal with. If a person runs off on you or doesn't respond to you in kind, they carry their own karma. You have nothing to worry about except your own attitude and vibration. Justice is always being maintained spiritually."

"Holy smokes," I say, shaking my head. "This is way outside my box. I've always picked sides and held grudges, especially when I see what I think is injustice."

"And what you're saying, Nicole, is that by doing this, we're only hurting ourselves and our relationships," Judy says.

Nicole nods and looks lovingly at her husband.

"This almost cost us our marriage," Jordan says quietly. "At the time, I just didn't get it."

"Neither did I," Nicole says. "For whatever it's worth, we were like the blind leading the blind, both suffering from tremendous grief, which triggered anger and attack."

"Well, you two give us great hope," Judy offers. "There's a sense of peace and grace about you that I find magnetic."

I jump in. "I agree. You two have a flow and energy that I find mesmerizing."

Jordan laughs, shaking his head. "It's not for everyone, Jack. Remember, like vibes attract like vibes. There's a reason we're sitting here right now having this conversation with you. Not everyone would appreciate it."

Nicole reaches over and gently grabs her husband's hand. "Not everyone likes and appreciates Jordan," she says. "Of course, this is true for a lot of thought leaders and change agents."

Nicole is right. It reminds me of Kathleen's comment about Abraham Lincoln and Dr. Martin Luther King Jr. Great leaders seeking to pull people together are often persecuted by those who see things differently. And then I think of Jesus and the crucifixion. No wonder *ACIM* describes the ego as insane.

"I guess that's where the ego comes in, huh? The ego feels threatened by anyone with an authentic spiritual vibe."

Jordan smiles. "Yes, it does. You just can't let other people's negative attitudes change yours. This is what Jesus meant when he talked about vigilance. We must be vigilant about the Truth. And the Truth is all about love and peace and joy and forgiveness. It's about atonement. This is what we must protect. It's always present, and it's always available to us. We just have to wake up, see it, and embrace it, no matter what."

39

The Second Coming

Even the least among you can do all that I have done,
and greater things.

—**John 14:12**

I arrive in my office thirty minutes earlier than usual to meditate and contemplate. This is in addition to my morning swim, which also allows me to focus on my breathing and clear my head. I figure, what better way to start the day than in stillness and peace—along with a little exercise. Hopefully, I can carry this energetic frequency with me throughout the day.

I reflect on *ACIM*. If there is one thing made clear in the course, it's that our one true purpose in life is forgiveness. This is the key to happiness and salvation. This is the key to atonement. This is where healing and miracles flourish. We are here to forgive one another, and by forgiving others, we are forgiving ourselves. We are setting ourselves free to live life on earth as it is in heaven.

Nicole's comment about the second coming really made me stop and think. I was always led to believe that Jesus would come back someday and fix everything. Now I suppose that might suggest a third and a fourth coming, since the first one didn't seem to work. We're still screwing things up on this planet, and it's been over two thousand years.

I've never been much of a "wait and see" kind of guy. When I see something wrong, I want to fix it now. Maybe this explains why I've been so upset and angry much of my life. I focus on things that are wrong, and I expect them to be fixed, according to my perception and judgment. Of course, that's my perception and judgment. Obviously, a lot of other people see things differently. Just look at our government. It's more divisive than most high school cliques. We have a whole national culture of divisiveness and separation, us versus them, all driven by the ego. Whatever happened to the third right answer?

Pulling everyone together is more than a one-person job, even if it is Jesus leading the way. We need to do this together. We need to wake up collectively and see beyond the ignorant ego thought-system, the root cause to all problems. The ego just loves it when we fight and debate and threaten one another. The drama is juicy and exciting. Peace, on the other hand, is boring for most people. We say we want it, but then we struggle taking ten minutes to meditate and see the light of heaven in the mind's eye.

I reaffirm my commitment to miracle-minded management at TYPCO. I know this won't be easy, and I may be scorned for leading something so outrageous in corporate America. But I'm going to do it. Just like I'm going to invest in Maximum's Brewery. I'm no longer afraid to step outside my own comfort zone, my own box, and pursue things that my heart gives me reason for. I see now that fear is indeed a self-created illusion.

Jordan has found a way to build miracle-minded management into his consulting practice, and he's obviously very successful. He doesn't call it miracle-minded management, just like Jesus didn't coin the term *Christianity*. He simply embodies it. He demonstrates it with every move he makes. If I do the same thing with my leadership team and reinforce it with the training I am developing with Georgia, we will ultimately behave in a very different way. And I will hold people accountable. I can't say I'm going to do something and then not follow through. That would destroy my credibility.

This reminds me of the interviews we had with Larry. Like I promised, I had Georgia arrange for Larry to visit TYPCO and interview with HR, finance, and accounting. By the end of the day, everyone agreed to extend him an offer contingent upon our background checks. Why did our normal process miss this guy? And why does our normal process take so long? And how many other great candidates are out there, wondering what happened to their application at TYPCO? Georgia is now all over this, and we have another kaizen event planned for next month. We're going to blow up our existing recruiting process and come up with something entirely new and exciting. Miracle-minded management doesn't take months to do something that can be done in a day or two.

One of my top takeaways from *ACIM* so far is that we are all teachers and we are all students. There is no separation. We teach by demonstration—always and everywhere. People observe what we say and what we do, and they take note, consciously and subconsciously. As students, we learn not just from one another but from what we teach through our own demonstration. Therefore, we must be mindful and vigilant about what we think and what we do, especially with the law of karma in play. What goes around comes around.

TYPCO is obviously a work in process. I realize that now, more than ever. Yet I'm at peace with it. Before, I wanted things changed immediately and without thoughtfulness and intention. I was dwelling on everything that was wrong, and I expected action and accountability. This brought about a culture of fear, defensiveness, and blame. It also meant that we would often solve one problem in haste and create three more in the process. There was no systems-thinking and mindful coordination of activity. Rather than sounding like a symphony with harmony, timing, and balance, we sounded more like a band warming up—with everyone playing whatever they wanted.

My blood pressure is still high, but it's improving. And I'm dropping a lot of weight. I attribute this to several factors, beginning with more peace of mind. I simply don't get stressed like I used to. Don't get me wrong, I'm still tested. Quite frequently. Every day, in fact. But I'm getting better at managing the gap—the gap between stimulus and response. I'm more conscious and aware of this gap to begin with. And I'm doing a better job at choosing more positive responses. I used to be a "fire, ready, aim" guy. Now, I'm putting a lot more emphasis on mindfulness and readiness, carefully, before aiming and pulling the trigger.

I am also eating better. Sheila gave Judy and me some great tips on nutrition, so I'm a lot more conscious about what I put in my body. And how I shop for groceries. One tip was to buy foods where the only ingredient is the food itself. No additives. No preservatives. Like an avocado or a pepper or a bunch of spinach. She encouraged us to avoid things like sugar, artificial sweeteners, and processed foods, including processed carbs. She suggested we eat a healthy amount of "good" fat, like coconut oil and wild fish and nuts. Apparently, a low-fat diet is foolish. The body needs fat for energy, endurance, and brain power. It also needs good fat to process and eliminate bad fat. Go figure. I had that all wrong. Sheila also gave us a few recipes, including one for a morning smoothie, which is now part of my daily routine. It's loaded with healthy proteins, enzymes, greens, and fats—which gives me a nice boost before my swim or walk. I'm eating a scoop of sauerkraut every morning too. Sauerkraut is a healthy probiotic that keeps my gut clean and boosts my immune system. What a blessing Sheila turned out to be. A few simple changes, and I feel ten years younger.

I pick up my family photo from the credenza, the one of us at Breckenridge. Wow! I really am blessed. Despite the countless mistakes I've made, life is good. I'm still in the same place, working with the same people, and yet I feel much more at peace. I put the picture back on the credenza and pick up a new one I have added: a photo of my mom and dad. Mom is smiling in her gentle way, and Dad is standing there like he's having his picture taken for his driver's license. I laugh. I know that behind that grim face and stoic stance, there is holiness. There is a son of God. A beautiful soul. A man of love. And even though he has now moved on from physical form, I feel closer to him than ever before. I whisper, "Thank you," and set the picture down. Let me bring peace to everyone I encounter today.

Epilogue

Let Go and Let Flow

Stand before it and there is no beginning. Follow it and there is no end. Stay with the Tao, move with the present.

—Lao Tzu

It's been a little over a year now since Judy and I completed *ACIM*. I really enjoyed taking the course with her. It gave us so much to talk about and integrate into our relationship. She is quietly practicing miracle-minded management at the hospital and cherishing the positive reactions she is getting from her colleagues. A few people have asked her what her secret is, and she is open to sharing it when asked. I am doing the same thing at TYPCO. We now have a very thoughtful leadership development course in play with key miracle-minded principles as its foundation. It has helped us clarify and articulate our leadership vision, values, and expectations, which has also helped us align our team members. Now, it is crystal clear what is expected from people who sign on with TYPCO, and we are using this focus and alignment to accelerate our growth. It's making things a lot easier too.

Today, Jordan and Nicole have invited Judy and me out to their beach house on the Cape. It's been a few months since we've all been together, so we're excited to reunite. We always seem to have so much to talk about, and Judy and I generally walk away feeling somewhat enlightened. Hopefully, they do too.

When we arrive at the McKays', we find a quaint Cape Cod house with gray shingles and purple shutters resting on a small sand dune and surrounded by tall beach grass. The ocean view is spectacular, and the lush gardens encircling the house are stunning. The daffodils, rhododendrons, and azaleas are in full bloom, and it appears the hydrangeas and hibiscus are next. We sit on a beautiful stone patio, and Nicole brings out a tray of iced tea and lemonade.

"I can see where you get some of your Zen, Jordan," I say, pointing at the azaleas bursting with color. "It's so peaceful here."

He smiles. "Well, it goes both ways, Jack. Gardens respond well to love, peace, and positive energy."

Judy turns to Jordan. "Correct me if I'm wrong, but isn't that one of the central themes in the course?"

"It is. And gardening is a nice way to practice it. Nic and I put a lot of Zen into our gardens, and they respond in kind. That's the essence of flow. By giving, we receive."

"And it's a great way to connect with the earth," Nicole adds. "Have you two been Earthing?"

Judy kicks off her sandals and plants both feet on the stone. "We started immediately after doing our research," she replies. "We bought a grounded bedsheet. You were right. The science is compelling. And yet so many people are not even aware of it. I find it amazing how infrequently people touch the earth with their skin these days."

I look down at my own feet and quickly kick off my shoes. Jordan laughs.

For the next twenty minutes, Judy and I share a few stories about using miracle-minded management at work. I describe how we're building it into our culture at TYPCO in a more formal way, and Judy gives examples of how she is using it in more subtle ways at the hospital. Jordan and Nicole seem genuinely intrigued.

"You know something, Jack," he says. "You've given me some great ideas. Thank you."

Ha! Imagine that. The student is teaching the professor. "Like what?" I ask, now wondering what I said.

"Like designing miracle-minded management tenets into a formal leadership-development process. I don't know of any other companies doing things quite this way."

I look at Judy and then back at Jordan. "Can I take that as a compliment?"

He smiles. "If your ego needs a compliment, be my guest."

We both laugh. "I should have known better," I chuckle.

"And I really like the term *miracle-minded management*," Jordan continues. "The more I think about it, the more it grows on me. It's unique. It's innovative. And it sends a radically different message to managers everywhere."

"Well, you know, you've been using miracle-minded management with me for years. You just didn't call it that."

He nods and sips his tea. "Thank you. My ego accepts that as a compliment."

Again, we laugh. It's amazing now to see the ego as almost a third person. It wants credit. It wants compliments. It wants us to attach to it and identify with it, but with a healthy amount of awareness and mindfulness, we begin to see that we are so much more than that. Why limit oneself with such little, insecure thinking?

"I have a question for you two," Judy says, looking at Jordan and then Nicole. "This has had me wondering for a long time."

She sips her lemonade. "Why don't more people understand this? I mean, it's not like it's new."

Jordan glances at Nicole. "You want to take this one, Nic?"

"Sure," she says as if they're in perfect sync. "It's probably the question of the millennium. In one word, I would say the answer is paradox. True knowledge in life requires understanding paradoxes that can be very confusing, even blinding."

"You mean, like we're often blinded by paradigms, our mental boxes?" Judy questions.

"Yes." Nicole explains. "They go hand in hand. We believe in certain paradigms that restrict us from understanding the wisdom of paradox. For example, we may be conditioned to think that to *have* more, we need to *get* more. We need to stock up and keep adding. This puts us in a taking mode. What else can we get? The truth is just the opposite. To have more, we need to give more. This is the paradox. This is what so many people don't understand."

"Because it doesn't seem to make sense," Judy concludes. "It doesn't fit the ego paradigm. How am I supposed to have more if I give everything away?"

"Precisely," Nicole says. "This makes no sense to the ego. Another confusing paradox is that to truly succeed and feel free in life, we need to surrender. We need to let go to let flow. To the ego this is seen as weak."

"We need to surrender the ego, right?" I ask. "Surrender to a higher power."

"Yes," she explains. "However, this is the last thing the ego wants you to believe. Think of it like the fox guarding the chickens. The ego's survival depends on our attachment to it. In Truth, it's all an illusion."

The meek shall inherit the earth, I think, reflecting on the words of Jesus.

"Here are two more paradoxes to contemplate," Nicole says. "To accomplish more, we must do less. And to move faster, we must slow down."

"I certainly have struggled with these," I admit. "I've always been programmed to believe that to be successful, I have to work hard . . . and a lot . . . and fast! If I want something done right, I need to do it myself. If I want something for myself and my family, I have to earn it. I need to take it. Miracles might be something people talk about on Sunday and pray about when someone is sick. But in my world, there is no time for this idealistic thinking. It's up to me to take charge and make things happen. It's 'my will be done,' not 'Thy will be done.'"

"Well, you certainly aren't alone, Jack," Nicole says. "That's common human nature."

Judy reaches over and grabs my hand, giving me a gentle squeeze. "Yet if we've learned anything from the course, it's that our true nature is spiritual, not human. Our human experience is temporary. Our spiritual existence is eternal. And it's only that which is eternal that is real."

"Yes, that's the essence of the course," Nicole says. "And nothing real can be threatened."

"Herein lies the peace of God," I add, squeezing my wife's hand.

Nicole smiles and looks at Jordan. "Yes, herein lies the peace of God."

Jordan raises his iced tea in the air, as if to make a toast. "And knowing this makes all the difference in the world."